Entrepreneurial Freedom

*How To Start and Grow
A Profitable Virtual Assistance Practice*

Second Edition

by
Jeannine Clontz and Lauren Hidden

Copyright © 2011 by Jeannine Clontz and Lauren Hidden. All rights reserved.

No part of this book may be reproduced or transmitted in any form or by any means, electronic or mechanical, including photocopying, recording or by any information storage and retrieval system without permission in writing from the copyright owner – except by a reviewer who may quote brief passages in a review to be printed in a magazine, newspaper, or posted on the Web.

For information, please contact:
Jeannine Clontz
Biz-E Press – 636-282-9550
Jeannine@Accbizsvcs.com

Entrepreneurial Freedom: How to Start and Grow a Profitable Virtual Assistance Practice, 2nd edition
Edited by: Lauren Hidden
Layout by: Diane Mendez
Cover Design by: Studio H
Printed in the U.S.A. by: CreateSpace.com

This book contains detailed information about starting and growing your small business. We are not attorneys or CPA's and do not represent ourselves as such anywhere in this book. We encourage you to seek the assistance of such professionals when setting up and implementing your business, where applicable.

Publisher's Cataloging-in-Publication
(Provided by Quality Books, Inc.)

    Clontz, Jeannine.
      Entrepreneurial freedom : how to start and grow a
    profitable virtual assistance practice / by Jeannine
    Clontz and Lauren Hidden. – 2nd ed.
      p. cm.
      Includes bibliographical references and index.
      ISBN-13: 978-0-9785941-3-8
      ISBN-10: 0-9785941-3-4

      1. Administrative assistants. 2. Virtual reality in management. 3. Home-based businesses. 4. New business enterprises. I. Hidden, Lauren. II. Title.

    HF5547.5.C58 2011   651.3'068'1
                                  QBI10-600224

Library of Congress Control Number: 2010917101

Praise for Entrepreneurial Freedom

"Entrepreneurial Freedom is the book I wish I'd had when I started my company! Clontz and Hidden have created a complete, step-by-step roadmap for starting and growing a successful VA practice, including firsthand advice from industry veterans, an overview of required skills and equipment, a process for determining rates, proven marketing techniques, and sample contracts and forms. Their advice is motivational, cutting-edge, reliable, and easy to follow. The authors give their readers a gentle but firm push in the right direction, such that Entrepreneurial Freedom is an excellent resource for anyone considering a career in virtual assistance."

–Heather Lee, Principal - design/type

"Entrepreneurial Freedom doesn't make pie-in-the-sky promises to its readers about how easy it is to start and run a VA business, like some VA how-to books do. It cuts to the chase, offering specific advice on how to get and keep clients, communicate with prospective and current customers, and behave in a professional manner while setting reasonable boundaries. This book contains a wealth of resources for business development and insightful perspectives from veteran VA's."

–Nina Feldman, Nina Feldman Connections, consultant
An Expense and Time Worksheet to Help Determine Billing Rate

"Wow, what a long and informational read that I highly recommend to anyone starting up a virtual business but specifically those who are thinking of becoming a VA! This took me longer to read than I first anticipated since it was surpassingly thorough and contained heaps of valuable business startup information. I didn't want to skim through any part of it! This is an excellent source for any new or seasoned Virtual Assistant which will surely be referenced time and time again. It gives you all the practical information needed to get started as a Virtual Assistant including helpful samples documents and contracts. The bonus links and resources at the end of each chapter are a handy addition to this book making future referencing simple and easily available when needed. 166 pages of Virtual Assistant success!"

Tawnya Sutherland, a Certified Internet Marketing Specialist, is the Founder of VAnetworking.com and Author of The Virtual Business Startup System, for aspiring and successful Virtual Assistants.

"This book has been around for a while—it was first published in 2006—but the information is all still relevant. Jeannine Clontz is a respected businesswoman who served as President of the International Virtual Assistants Association and Lauren Hidden has owned her own virtual editorial services business for over ten years, so these are authors who know the world of which they speak, and as such, are able to offer advice and guidance in areas not always explored by other **"How-To Freelance"**-type books. Sure, you'll find more typical discussions of topics such as how to decide if this is the career for you and the financial investment you'll need to start up your business, but what made me a fan were the more "experience based" topics like how to get rid of clients or turn down jobs. As someone who has gained a reputation as an expert in the area through speaking engagements and writing Clontz, especially, understands the topic of business ethics through and through. **What types of jobs are you not willing to do? How far will you go for a buck?** Again, not your typical how-to fare, but in a business in which the projects and jobs we take on are all a result of our choices, these are decisions we're all going to have to examine.

Another invaluable part of this book is the resources referenced and given throughout. **Not only are helpful Web sites and resources handed out like yummy candy in each chapter, there's a whole section in the back on contracts.** Not on what they are or how to implement them, though that's all explained, too—no, what we have here are actual template contracts for subcontractor agreements, work for hire agreements, editorial retainer agreements, client retainer agreements, non-solicitation agreements, confidentially agreements, and even a business plan. These are great not only to show you how to do the contracts, but to teach you specifics of what you need to look for even if you **DON'T** go with a formal agreement.

Though I wouldn't necessarily consider myself a Virtual Assistant in the truest sense of the word, a lot of my projects aren't strictly writing, so I've often thought about just calling myself a VA and embracing the bigger picture. I read **Entrepreneurial Freedom: How to Start and Grow a Profitable Virtual Assistance Practice** by Jeannine Clontz and Lauren Hidden in the hopes of trying to pinpoint exactly what being a Virtual Assistant entailed, but as it turned out, not only does the book encompass pretty much any type of freelancing work you might be doing, it makes an often misconstrued profession seem absolutely construed."

FreelanceWeekly.com (6/24/2010)

This book is dedicated to:

All those aspiring, talented, hard-working people who are looking for a profitable work-from-home option that will provide them with a good income and more flexibility. You'll find that running your VA business gives you the freedom to spend more time with your children or family, learn new skills, travel, volunteer, or indulge in your favorite hobby or sport—all the things that are so difficult to manage in the 8-5 corporate world.

And to all those people we have mentored throughout the years, or who called or put service requests through our websites under the guise of a potential client, just to find out about our pricing; to all those who glibly say, 'I can type, I can be a VA!"; and most importantly, to all those who are already living the dream—whether for one year or twenty-five years, and truly aspire to greatness; we dedicate this book.

The Virtual Assistance industry is in its infancy, and suffers, as almost all industries do, with growing pains, business owners who are pains, and providers and clients who are less-than-ethical in their practices. We challenge you all to consider the information and guidance offered in the pages of our book to help you and your colleagues develop a strong and viable 'virtual' industry.

With a good dose of planning, lots of hard work, and facing your fears, you CAN make your dream of having your own business a reality. We can attest to the rewards, fulfillment and freedoms that being a successful virtual business owner can mean for you and your family.

Let us help you take your first steps to finding the courage to make your dream a reality. YOU CAN DO IT!

Acknowledgements

I couldn't possibly begin an acknowledgment without acknowledging my co-author, Lauren Hidden. Lauren contacted me a month into my term as President of the International Virtual Assistants Association (www.ivaa.org), at a time when I was still trying to manage a schedule that included running my own VA practice, helping my husband with a start-up business, running our household, volunteering for three other organizations, and devoting about 15-20 hours a week to the care and feeding of IVAA.

I thought this woman had lost her mind, how could I possibly write a book in the midst of this chaotic life? But somehow we did, and with her encouragement, and calming support, she helped make the book you are about to read a reality, one I had often considered, but never dreamed could be accomplished.

My husband, Neil and daughter, Nicole were very understanding throughout this year long adventure, and helped me to maintain just a small portion of my sanity, while reveling in the fact that it was amazing that a human being could survive on so little sleep for so long! ;) I could not have considered starting or completing this book had it not been for their support.

Who could not acknowledge their parents as the people who inspired them to do great things? I am no exception. My Dad, although lost to us for more than ten years, truly made all nine of us independent thinkers with the drive and desire to find our own path, work hard to get there, and always stand up for what we believe. Mom provides the support and guidance, and of course, the inspiration, to not take life so seriously, but to enjoy God's gifts and use those gifts to help ourselves and others lead long and happy lives. She is a wonderful role model and cheerleader for all her children, grandchildren and great grandchildren. How could we not aspire to do great things?

To my mentor, the late Don Earl, who taught me so much about being an entrepreneur, and the wonderful world of volunteering. He helped me to develop patience, understanding, and gave me the spirit and spirituality that has helped to make me a success. I miss you every single day!

I must also thank the many bright and talented people who have shared their insights and knowledge to allow us to look at all angles of running a VA practice, and the trials and tribulations that helped to make them successful. You will see their wisdom interspersed within these pages and understand their true power and passion for our industry. They are: Katy Baird, Barbie Dallmann, Lori Davis, Vicki Duncan, Jackie Eastwick, Nina Feldman, Sandy Giusti, Michele Hanson-O'Reggio, Lisa Hoffman, Heather Jacobson, Sue Kramer, Heather Lee, Judy Ann Lorenz, Kathy Mandy, Marlene McCall, Faye Partridge, Linda Siniscal, Kimberley Thomas-Catanzaro, Judy Vorfeld, Marsha Wagner, Sharon Williams, Janice Wlodarski, and Caroline Wright. Although many of us are separated by thousands of miles and even a couple of oceans, I am privileged to call them friend. Some have been friends and colleagues for many years, while others have just recently touched my life.

And finally, I fondly recall my second year in business, a time when I thought I just couldn't make it, that I just wasn't savvy enough to run my own business, and I was about to give up. Three local pioneers I met through a St. Louis based networking group, Office Support Network, saw something in me that I didn't. They pushed me to continue to fight to take my business to the next level, to turn the corner and become a success story. Without these cheerleaders, I would not be here today writing an acknowledgement to a labor of love that I hope will inspire others to take the first step in making their dream a reality. I thank Kay Young, Beth Quick-Andrews, and Margie Robinson for always being there to encourage and support me when I needed it most. Thank you, thank you, thank you ALL!

Jeannine Clontz

Acknowledgements

My first thank you goes to Jeannine Clontz, my co-author. After co-authoring my first book, Write It Right: The Ground Rules for Self-Editing Like the Pros, I was speaking at a writers' conference and asked what my next book was going to be. That started the ball rolling. At the time, I felt the VA industry could use a good printed book on how to start and run your own VA practice. I asked Jeannine if she was interested in co-authoring a book with me and she graciously agreed. I'm not quite sure how she fit it in with her insanely busy schedule, but I'm glad she did. Jeannine was a fabulous president during her terms at IVAA and I have learned so much from her through writing this book and the years we've known each other.

To all the VAs I've met through IVAA and other organizations who have always been there as a sounding board and a source of support. I hope that through volunteering with these associations, I am giving back at least a small portion of what I've gained.

To Dawn Josephson, who has been my friend and business mentor for many years. Thank you for giving me my first virtual work back in 2000 before either of us had heard of the term, "virtual assistant."

To my parents, Frank and Barbara Davis who regularly tell me how proud they are of me, which I never tire of hearing.

To my children, Kyle and Andrew, who make me thankful everyday that I picked such a flexible career.

To my husband, Ed, the artist behind The Hidden Helper. Thanks for being my website designer, graphic artist, and tech support person.

To my clients, who trust me, value my services, and don't micromanage me. Without them, I would not be able to have this dream career. Thank you.

Lauren Hidden

Table of Contents

Introduction 15

CHAPTER ONE
Do You Have What It Takes? 17
What You Need For Your VA Business 18
   Capital 18
   Will You Need Retail Space? 20
   What's Your Experience? 20
   Can You Persevere? 21
   Are You Self-Confident? 21
   Are You Outgoing? 22
   The Executive Summary 23
   Chapter Links and Resources 24

CHAPTER TWO
Planning Your Business 25
   Part-time v. Full-time 25
   Your Shopping List 27
   A Business Phone 27
   Hardware 28
   Software 28
   A Printer 29
   Other Communications Equipment 29
   Bookkeeping Software 30
   Considering Options to Organize Your Company 30
   Business Plans 31
   Contracts and Forms 33
   Record Keeping 34
   Delegating Business Tasks 34
   The Executive Summary 35
   Start-Up Options At-A-Glance 35
   Chapter Links and Resources 37

CHAPTER THREE
Branding 39
   Naming Your Business 39
   Taglines 40
   30-Second Commercials 41
   Creating a Website 42
   Website Guidelines 43
   Rates: To List or Not to List? 44
   Getting Set Up On the World Wide Web 46
   Signature Lines 49
   Setting Your Fees 50
   Setting "A" Client Criteria 52
   Tracking Client Time and Time Management 54
   Professional Image 56

The Executive Summary	58
Chapter Links and Resources	59
Sample Taglines	62

CHAPTER FOUR
How to Find and Keep Clients ... 63
Networking Groups Online and Off	63
Social Media Networks	65
How Exactly Do You Network?	66
Taking Networking One Step Further	67
Overcoming Client Objections	68
Price	68
Working Virtually	69
Timing	70
Communicating With Clients	71
Handling Difficult Clients	72
Local Businesses Versus Virtual Clients	73
Ethics and Customer Service	74
Saying "No" To a Potential Client	75
Firing Clients	76
Collections	77
The Executive Summary	78
Chapter Links and Resources	79

CHAPTER FIVE
Professional Development ... 81
Continuing Education	81
Industry and Small Business Conferences	83
Certifications	84
Professional Associations	85
Books	86
The Web	87
Podcasts	87
Blogs	87
The Executive Summary	88
Chapter Links and Resources	89

CHAPTER SIX
Marketing, Advertising & Public Relations ... 91
Marketing	91
Paid Advertising	91
Consider Bartering	92
How Do You Know What Works?	92
Keep Track of Your Results	92
Word of Mouth Marketing	93
How to Get Free Publicity	94
Sales	95
Giveaways	96
Social Media & Bookmarking	97
The Executive Summary	105
Chapter Links and Resources	106

CHAPTER SEVEN
The Challenges of Working From Home 109
   Balancing Work and Home 109
   Scheduling and Boundaries 109
   Handling Isolation 112
   Handling Small Children 113
   The Executive Summary 114
   Chapter Links and Resources 115

CHAPTER EIGHT
Ethical Considerations 117
   Accurately Representing your Experience and Capabilities 118
   Keeping Client Files Safe 119
   Maintaining Confidentiality 120
   The Executive Summary 122
   Chapter Links and Resources 122

CHAPTER NINE
Growing Your Business 125
   Adding Staff 125
   How to Effectively Work With Subcontractors 126
   Qualify Your Subs 127
   Multi-VA Practice 128
   When You Need to Hire Others 129
   When You Need to Move Out of Your Home Office 130
   Growth Doesn't Always Involve Volume 131
   Go Deeper Into A Niche 131
   Become A Leader 132
   Teach Others How to Become Successful 132
   The Executive Summary 133
   Chapter Links and Resources 134

Epilogue: The Battle of Being a VA 135

Survey Results 139

Survey Participant Bios 143

Sample Documents 149

About the Authors 175

Index 179

Introduction

*S*everal years ago, when someone would ask us what we do for a living, the response "I'm a virtual assistant" would bring a puzzled expression rather than an understanding one. But times are changing, and if people don't currently know what a virtual assistant is, they soon will. Virtual Assistance has become a much more recognized and respected career option for busy entrepreneurs in many industries.

As the business world becomes more technology-savvy, remote working isn't just a possibility; it's a probability. Many things that once required an administrative assistant sitting just outside their boss's office can now be done remotely from home. Email, instant messaging, economical business telephone plans and even webcams can shrink the distance from remote locations.

Virtual assistants have the benefit of years of experience, specialized expertise and, in most cases, low overhead. This can greatly benefit businesses or entrepreneurs who have specialized, occasional, or limited needs for assistance. The VA benefits from having a more flexible work schedule, a higher income, and, with practice, a work/life balance that so many people are struggling to achieve.

Starting a virtual assistant business is not something to be taken lightly. Like any worthwhile endeavor, it will take time, skill, persistence, and a few mistakes along the way. If you have "virtual assistance" on your mind, whether you're just thinking of becoming a VA, still in the start-up phase, or have your own well-established business, this book will give you the tools and insider's knowledge to help get, (and keep) your practice running, evolving, and thriving in the shortest time possible.

To help give you a more personal insight into what it's like to be a VA, we surveyed more than 20 successful virtual assistants in different levels and types of practices and their quotes will be sprinkled throughout the book. We appreciate them taking the time to answer our questions and have included their business and contact information, as well as a recap of what we learned from them, at the back of the book.

We developed the content of this book in response to questions and issues most frequently asked by VAs and through the 'school of hard knocks' that we have faced in developing our own successful practices. By reading this book, you are taking one successful step in a series of many in running your own successful, profitable and rewarding virtual assistance business.

With the dramatic changes in technology, the way virtual assistants work, and the new options for VA support, we felt it would be important that we update our book, this Second Edition, as a natural part of the on-going process to keep the information fresh, and up-to-date with the changing trends and needs of the industry. We hope you will enjoy the latest additions as you consider your options for a successful business adventure.

CHAPTER ONE

Do You Have What It Takes?

*A*rguably, a virtual assistant practice is easier to start up than many other businesses. It doesn't cost tens of thousands of dollars, and it shouldn't take you too many years to break even. But this doesn't mean you should underestimate the effort involved—starting up a VA business requires an investment of time, blood, sweat, and tears to get your practice off the ground and then to keep it profitable (and enjoyable) for the long haul.

The Internet is filled with people looking for work from home opportunities. It's also a playground for scam artists. Some people are so desperate to work from home that they get suckered into unscrupulous business "opportunities." Others, with the best of intentions, decide that being a virtual assistant is an easy way to make a living and jump into it without spending the time to investigate whether or not it's a good fit for them. But starting your VA business isn't a "get rich quick" opportunity, and to be successful, it's going to require the same dedication a "regular" business start-up would require.

The recent turn of the economy has provided our industry with a blessing and a curse of sorts. The blessing comes in the form of increased interest in what a virtual professional brings to the mix as it relates to providing organizations with 'as-needed' professional support without the exposure to taxes and expenses required of in-house staff. After being forced to cut back on staff through lay-offs, many new prospects are now looking at VAs as a viable option to fill-in the areas where cutbacks have forced middle to upper management to take on additional workload that many times gets left on the back burner, or never again sees the light of day.

> *"My experience in the corporate world helped greatly. There I learned how the business climate works, what hard work looks like, how to communicate and work with different levels of management and staff."*
>
> Janice Wlodarski,
> Progressive Publishing Services

The curse comes in the form of the massive numbers of people who were laid off or downsized during this time who don't realize the needs of establishing a viable business model, but simply put their hats in the ring to do project work. This has in some cases 'muddied the waters' of our industry, in that these providers, while they have the expertise/skills to perform the work, don't have the entrepreneur's mindset necessary to maintain and grow the business. This then leaves less than stellar customer service and potential clients who discontinue the use of VAs due to the dissatisfaction and lack of business knowledge portrayed by these pseudo-VAs, hurting our industry.

For those who are willing to get the business knowledge and expertise necessary to develop a Virtual Assistance practice, they find a much easier road to climb, and help to solidify the overall perception of the industry. Since you are reading this book, we must believe you are willing to look at establishing a solid foundation for your VA practice.

> "...Making people feel comfortable and secure with me was the most important thing in obtaining clients. Face it, no matter how good you are, if you can't get clients, your business will not get off the ground."
>
> Jackie Eastwick,
> Allison Lane Business Solutions

On the upside, a virtual assistant practice is very flexible. You have the ability to work from home, set your own hours and set your own rates. Unlike opening a franchise or a brick and mortar business, you won't need to work 16-hour days and need to be physically present for your customers at all times. However, opening a VA practice will require your time, money and energy and will affect the rest of your family, too. Being a VA can be a dream come true for some, and a living nightmare for others. Read on to take an objective look at whether you have what it takes to be a happy and successful virtual assistant.

What You Need For Your VA Business

To start up your virtual assistance practice, you need to possess some tangible items and some intangible traits. The following is a list of some items to consider before starting your VA business.

Capital

Starting your business will take some cold, hard, cash, (or at least a credit card or loan). How much money you need depends on many factors—what specialties you want to work in, how top-of-the-line you want or need your equipment to be, and what initial level of monetary exposure you are comfortable with. Carefully evaluate your wants versus needs for a practice and make a list of your bare minimum expenses and your money-is-no-object ones.

If you are going to be home-based, minimally you can start a practice for about three thousand dollars. That will be enough for a computer, basic software and supplies to get things rolling. But, in reality, you will need to be able to fund your current lifestyle and pay your expenses for approximately two years. That will give you the ability to keep your household running smoothly while you establish and market your business. It could take anywhere from three to five years for your business to support itself in the manner that would allow you to draw a regular salary.

You may even find VAs who have been able to establish and grow their businesses much more quickly, so it is certainly possible, however, if you go into this endeavor with the understanding that in most cases it will take several years for you to draw a regular salary, you will alleviate some of the natural pressures owning a business creates.

> *"I'm an extrovert, but didn't realize how important that was going to be. I was vastly mistaken when I started my business thinking that most of my work would involve quietly working at the computer. I don't believe that being a VA is a good job for an extremely shy person to pursue."*
>
> Nina Feldman,
> Nina Feldman Connections

Want to start your business before you could save up that much money? It's still possible. There are many other ways to fund the start-up costs of your business. Here are some possibilities:

- Refinance your home
- Use your home's equity
- Borrow from friends or family
- Secure a personal loan based on collateral, stocks and bonds, mutual funds, etc.
- Use credit cards
- Sell personal or collectable properties
- Look to the Small Business Administration (SBA) for a loan
- Find an investor
- Apply for a business loan

Any of these options still give you the end result—capital to start your business.

Will You Need Retail Space?

If you're looking to plunge into retail space for your business, your capital needs will be higher and most likely require more structured funding. This will require you to get a business plan, financial statements and other paperwork in order before you can really walk into a bank and get your funding. Unless you really need retail space for your specific type of VA business, you may want to consider starting as a home-based business, and later moving it to rented office if you need to. The lower you can keep your overhead in the beginning, the sooner your business will be profitable.

> *"Strong customer service background, courage to take risks, excellent written communication skills (for use in initial marketing literature), ability to listen to others and learn from them, and to also continually learn from my failures."*
> Marlene McCall,
> Creative Office Services

What's Your Experience?

Very few jobs prepare you for running your own business and the leap from employee to entrepreneur is huge. You need two skill sets:

- entrepreneurial "know how"
- the specific skills required of your business services

> *"A basic understanding of financial management; experience dealing with people of diverse backgrounds; excellent written and verbal communication skills were very helpful in getting my business off the ground."*
> Heather Lee, design/type

Your past experience may not be as important as your talent and business software skills, but your corporate experience can be helpful in providing you with a basic understanding of what it takes to run a business. Initially, you're going to be responsible for paying the bills, setting up vendors, marketing, sales and promotion, getting systems in place, creating promotional materials, setting up bookkeeping practices and a pricing schedule. We'll go into this in much more detail in future chapters. If you feel totally unqualified in one or two of these areas, you can also outsource some of these tasks as you start to secure business.

Obviously, you should possess excellent skills in the services you are providing. You need to communicate and be confident in delivering what you say you can. Clients will instantly know whether you know what you're talking about as you try to sell them on the advantages and benefits of outsourcing work to you. The more experienced you are, the easier it will be to close the sale. You will also need to understand and build good communication skills in order to work with the different personalities and backgrounds that your client base will include.

Having good customer service skills and business ethics will round out the necessary level of experience that will be the solid foundation for your new business.

Can You Persevere?

Operating a successful business requires time, sacrifice, and lots of hard work. There are no short-cuts or quick fixes. You are the only person that will be responsible and accountable for your success and/or failure. That's a scary realization for many people. Having your own business will require some creative thinking, and some long nights. But the rewards and benefits of persevering far outweigh the sacrifices you need to make to be successful.

Like any business, you will have gains and losses. You will not get every client you pitch to. You may lose a client to a competitor, you might have clients that are delinquent in paying you, or clients that try to micromanage you and drive you nuts. You can't take any of these negatives personally—you'll learn to develop a thicker skin. Most importantly, you must be able to persevere and have faith that the positives of running your VA business far outweigh the negatives. Stick with it.

> *"Office, bookkeeping and customer service skills were helpful in getting my business started, and my time as a temp enabled me to move easily from one client job to another. I used the book, Up Close & Personal, to help guide me."*
>
> Kimberley Thomas-Catanzaro, Bookkeeping & Secretarial Services

Building a strong network of peers and business associates will help you stay on track and persevere, long after your subconscious has made you question your decision to dive into this new adventure.

Are You Self Confident?

How you perceive yourself plays a huge role in your business success. If you don't feel good about yourself and your ability to provide top-notch services, you'll have a hard time closing the deal.

There will also be some times throughout the year when business will be slow or soft. Without a healthy dose of confidence in yourself and your business, you will struggle to succeed. Self-confidence comes from within and takes work to maintain. Just like we need to exercise and eat right to maintain good health, we need to keep a positive attitude and confidence in ourselves and our ability to run an ethical and profitable business.

> "Overall, flexibility is probably the most important skill – being able to grow, adapt to a changing business environment, and re-inventing services based on the latest technology have been extremely valuable."
>
> Vicki L. Duncan,
> Duncan Business Services, Inc.

As you read farther into this book, you will find many ways to help maintain and improve your self-confidence. Your experience and perseverance are also keys to improving your attitude and the way you perceive yourself. As you continue to organize and grow your business, your pride and accomplishments will go far to bolster and improve your self-confidence.

If self-confidence is a struggle for you, look to your friends, family and colleagues to give you a boost. Give yourself a pep talk in front of the mirror or standing in the shower. Consider taking a class at a local community college or continuing education center. Spend some time at the library or local book store and read up on the subject. Start a journal and write down your accomplishments, no matter how small. Do whatever it takes. You need to be your biggest cheerleader. This is especially true when approaching possible clients and implementing marketing strategies. If you don't believe in yourself, potential clients won't believe in you either, no matter how skilled you are at the services you offer.

Are You Outgoing?

Not everyone is born with an outgoing personality, but you will need to develop one to create a stable business. It's all too easy to "hide" behind your computer and only deal with people on the phone and via email, but to develop a successful business you need to get out there in the world, hang out where your clients do, and make valuable contacts. Networking is an important part of your business. If you don't have an outgoing personality, this will be more of a challenge.

> "In a prior role as president of a large union, I depended on marketing, negotiations, networking, listening and analytical skills. I promoted them as valuable assets clients could utilize for their own business growth."
>
> Sharon Williams,
> The 24-Hour Secretary

You'll have to step out of your comfort zone to develop this ability, but the more you do, the easier it becomes. Participate in a variety of activities that allow you to try out different ways of delivering your message or be among other business owners who will be delivering theirs. Learn from them so you can develop your own strong message. None of this happens if you don't get out there.

On a local level, you will be forced to do this face-to-face. Working virtually allows you some additional protection from feeling uncomfortable in your surroundings. Later in this book you will learn about the advantages and benefits of volunteering and donating your services. Involvement in general business and industry organizations will help you in developing a strong, outgoing personality and help improve your self-esteem. Practice, practice, practice.

The Executive Summary

Remember that every business professional you meet had to start at the beginning—just like you. Don't be afraid to ask questions and develop relationships with other VAs to help you to decide if you 'have what it takes,' or can develop the necessary skills to get what it takes, to start and build your VA business.

> "In my business plan I detailed this approach: work full-time for the first three years to acquire a part-time workload. Spend half of my time promoting, networking and testing administrative procedures, etc., and half my time working. It seemed like I was ALWAYS working and making very little money for the first three years."
>
> Katie Baird, Loose Ends

Be creative and innovative, find something that sets you apart from the rest, and be certain that owning your own business is a good fit for you. Starting your own business takes a lot of courage, requires flexibility and is a big risk. Running a thriving business is not easy, but can be extremely rewarding if you take the time to do it right.

Chapter Links and Resources

Small Business Administration   www.sba.gov

Financing
Businessfinance.com   Lendingtree.com

                                       Cba.ca (Canadian Bankers)

Business information   businessknowhow.com

Additional reading   amazon.com

Chapter Two

Planning Your Business

Beginning your VA practice will not happen overnight. Like any major undertaking in your life, it will require some advanced planning. Whether your business is one you operate from your own home, or a brick-and-mortar store, you still need to carefully plan the evolution of your business as the decisions you make now will affect your profitability, security, and happiness for years to come.

Assess all your resources, create a timeline and detail your plans. With all your cards on the table, you can create the best plan for your business, ensuring your success for the long haul.

Part-time v. full-time

One of the first decisions you need to make is whether you start a part-time or full-time VA practice. If at all possible, go full-time right off the bat. Working regular business hours during the day gives you plenty of time to network, develop your marketing materials and be available to respond to customer inquiries promptly. Diving into your practice full-time also shows potential customers that this is your livelihood and your business and you take your occupation seriously.

If you're like many others contemplating starting their VA practice, you may be tempted to start it part-time while you work your current full-time job. This is possible, but be aware of some of the challenges that come along with that choice. When you work part-time, you are usually not accessible to potential clients during regular business hours and you will require additional time to complete projects. After all, you'll only have a limited amount of time to devote to VA work and you will have less time to market your practice so it will grow.

These issues will make it much more difficult for you, as a part-time VA, to compete with full-time VAs. It will also make it more difficult to serve your clients in the manner they deserve. Your business will take much longer to become profitable, too. Add all these challenges to trying to run a household and hold down your full-time job and it's a recipe for stress.

Keep in mind, when you begin by running your business full-time, you will gain some tax advantages, build a reputation, and establish a more traditional business model. You will also have the freedom to set your own hours and work at your own pace. You will be able to keep track of your finances, research any specializations or additional education/certifications you need and get involved in the industry. Your goal should be to move your VA practice to full-time as soon as humanly possible.

> "Amazingly, I found a guy who ran a small business putting together PC clones, and he provided me with the use of my own computer, shared use of a printer, and a desk in his office space – in return for acting as his office manager. I did that for about nine months and then had enough money to buy my own equipment and in a few months more, moved into my own office space."
>
> Marlene McCall, Creative Office Services Third Hand Secretarial Service™

For some people, it's just not feasible to make the plunge to becoming a full-time VA right out of the starting gate. Instead of starting your own VA practice part-time, consider going full-time earlier by establishing yourself as a subcontractor to some more well-established VAs, and do freelance project work through sites such as guru.com elance.com. and oDesk.com. The work through these sites is often much more difficult to obtain, and pays less than you would charge if you had your own practice, but it will at least help you get your feet wet to find out if this is the right business for you, and whether or not you can expect to build a profitable business. Then you can start landing clients for yourself and increase your profits.

If you decide to start your VA practice part-time, you won't be alone. Many VAs have part-time VA practices. Some have even elected to keep their business part-time, as a form of secondary income that will allow them some freedom in being a stay-at-home parent, without the business ever needing to go full-time. For most, however, your goal will be to take your practice to full-time as soon as possible. Take as much of this part-time income as humanly possible and set it aside in your "I'm going to be my own boss soon" fund. Pick a date for when you will quit your day job. Writing down your goal and posting it where you can see it will give you that much more incentive to reach your goal within the deadline you set.

If you want to start your VA practice debt-free, save about two years worth of your current salary and take your VA practice full-time. This may take a while. Better yet, save some money from your full-time job too until you save enough to bank this amount before you start your practice to allow you to maintain your current lifestyle and provide additional funding for marketing your business.

Initially, much of your income (whether you're running your VA practice part-time or full-time), should go back into the business to continue to grow and market your practice. Full-time clients, (those who give you a set number of hours every day or week), will help you build a more solid and profitable business and take your business where it needs to go much more quickly. Working your business part-time makes it much more difficult to land your ideal clients—ones that give you ongoing business instead of quick, one-time projects.

> *"I started my business while working part-time so for me, I never felt that I was not going to succeed, it was just a matter of when I could run my business full-time. When I started to get client referrals, my business started to grow and I was able to leave my full-time job and devote the time I really needed to continue the growth of my company."*
>
> Linda Siniscal,
> Third Hand Secretarial Service™

If you've decided a full-time practice makes the most sense for you, refer to Chapter One on funding options for starting up your business. If you don't see any way to start your practice full-time, then save up as much money as quickly as possible, so you can dive into your practice head first when the time is right.

Your Shopping List

You probably already have some kind of home office set-up. You may even have some of the equipment you'll need. As you read through the following section, make a list of what equipment you have and what equipment you will still need to purchase. Then, start shopping for the necessary items you'll need to get your practice started. Once you establish this budget, you will have a clear picture of your start-up costs.

A Business Phone

The most important piece of equipment you will need for your business is a separate telephone and telephone line. Even if you're going to start out part-time, and you really love the voice mail message your daughter "Susie" has on your answering machine, it is not appropriate for a business. No one will take you seriously if they call you at 3:30 in the afternoon and get a teenager who tells you they're on the other line, and to call back later because he doesn't want to take a message.

You can purchase a reasonably-priced basic telephone system that has a built-in answering machine, or add a phone to your current cell phone plan... just make sure you have a separate line (and number) for business calls only.

Whichever system you decide on, pick a unique ring for your business line so you'll always know which line someone is calling on and how to answer the phone. Take time in recording your voice mail message. Don't forget to smile when you're speaking. If it takes more than one attempt to have it sound right, that's okay. You need your professional voice mail message to match the professionalism of your company. You'll learn more about how to do this in upcoming chapters.

> *"As soon as I started my business, I turned our personal and business taxes over to a CPA for annual tax preparation and filing. Other than that, I handled – and continue to handle – most issues myself."*
>
> Heather Lee, design/type

Hardware

The other fundamental needs of a VA practice include, minimally, an up-to-date PC computer system, the most widely-used operating system, unless you are going to specialize in an area that requires lots of graphics, which may require a Mac computer system. You'll need an operating system of Windows XP, or higher, but preferably Windows XP or equivalent Basic software would include: MSOffice, (home edition at a minimum, professional version is even better). Some markets still utilize Corel products, but unless you know for sure your clients will use this software, don't purchase it right away.

Software

You will need to be sure that your software is compatible with your clients' software or you will not be able to communicate projects easily. If you are specializing in desktop publishing, additional software packages may be necessary, such as InDesign or Quark, but they are much more expensive, and not as widely used in most businesses. Although you can provide drafts and proofs via PDF, it still may prevent you from securing business with clients who want to maintain some control and use of the work product you create. If you don't have the software, you can't modify the project. This is another case where you may want to wait to see what your clients require before purchasing.

If you have the funding, and are considering a graphic design specialty, then software like Adobe Illustrator, Photoshop, and the full version of Adobe Acrobat may be necessary. Please note that these software programs are more expensive and less user friendly than Microsoft products. You may require additional training on these programs to have the ability to work within these environments.

A Printer

A basic inkjet (color) and laser-jet (black) printer are a must. You can initially start with an inkjet, which will be less costly, or just a laser-jet if you do not believe you will have a need to produce color projects, but even to do your own brochures will most likely require a color printer of some sort. Prices have come way down on color laser-jet printers, so if you have the budget, this may be the way to go. If you don't expect to be printing anything out that needs to look ultra-professional, you have the option of just buying an inkjet and outsourcing any print projects to a professional printing service.

Other Communications Equipment

You'll need a basic scanner, and fax equipment. This can consist of either a free-standing fax machine, fax software for your computer, or you can purchase an online fax service that delivers faxes directly to your e-mail account.

While all-in-one machines are popular because of their compact size and relative low-price, they are problematic for many VAs. If one of the functions stops working, it may affect all the other functions. Now instead of just your fax machine being down, so are your scanner and your printer. Is that a risk you want to take?

A small copier would also be a nice addition for your office. For multiple copies, a small copier is less expensive to run than printing the same number of copies from your laser-jet or inkjet. It will also allow you to make copies more reasonably as a cost-center to clients. At an entry-level price point, you can purchase a tabletop copier for a few hundred dollars. Keep in mind, though, they are not designed to make lots of copies, so be sure that you check the average monthly copies the machine is capable of before purchasing.

> *When we first started we handled EVERYTHING. Now we have a business attorney, payroll service, CPA, HR service, a bank contact person, and an attorney who specializes in personnel issues."*
>
> Vicki L. Duncan, Duncan Business Services, Inc.

As your company grows and so does your need for copies, you will want to check into a used copier, available through many local copier repair companies, or check out a local printer or copy shop. Of course, there are the Kinko's and CopyMax type places, but they usually do not give you much room for profit if you are making copies for clients, and driving or walking there to make the copies. This chore takes up billable hours that you cannot recoup.

If you're specializing in transcription, you'll need some digital software and/or transcription machines in the two basic cassette tape sizes: standard and micro. Most transcription is digital today, so look into computer foot pedals, and other reasonably priced online systems that allow your client to record dictation and you to download the necessary files. Please see the end of this chapter for resources on online options, as well as used transcription machines.

Bookkeeping Software

Finally, and as important as your telephone, some sort of Financial Software Package like QuickBooks. This program allows you to invoice clients and keep track of all the costs and expenses of running a business. Without some sort of software to track clients, sales, income and expenses, filing taxes, and getting paid by clients will be much more difficult to juggle.

Consider Options to Organize Your Company

Your virtual assistant business isn't just about you making money on the side, it's a true business, and it needs to be set up as one, by law. This is for your protection as well as your client's. The IRS laws continue to change as it relates to home-based businesses. Without an established business checking account, in some cases, the IRS may look at your services as those of an employee rather than an independent contractor leaving your clients exposed to employment taxes and insurance. This could seriously hurt your business, and theirs.

There are several different ways to organize your business. Schedule an appointment with a lawyer and/or a good CPA to discuss your options. Here are some brief overviews of some options to consider.

The easiest, least expensive way to organize your business is as a Sole Proprietor. You should contact your local City or County government to get all the details, but most Sole Proprietors simply need a company name and a State Registration of Fictitious Name in order to be setup to do business. This type of company is really still connected to you personally, although you can get an EIN (Employer Identification Number) in lieu of giving out your Social Security Number. Your profits or losses are usually claimed on your personal income tax returns, and although you do have some tax write-off advantages, you also bear personal responsibility if you are sued for any reason.

An LLC (Limited Liability Company) is a company whose liabilities are limited to what you have invested in the LLC. This means, if someone sues you, they can not recover any of your personal assets (like your house, personal savings account, etc.). The IRS views this type of organization the same way it views a partnership.

Corporations truly have the best benefits, but are much harder and more costly to establish. There are two forms of corporations: an S Corp, and a C Corp. In an S Corp, income passes through to you individually. With a C Corp, a straight corporation, any year-end income is taxed at the corporate level, and then taxed again on a personal level.

Most VAs start out as a Sole Proprietorship. Seek the guidance of your CPA or a corporate attorney for more information about the process and cost of each option along with the pros and cons for your unique needs. Find the best option and base your decision on your needs and the laws in your area.

Business Plans

Business plans are a must. Do not start your business without having a basic business plan in place. Be sure that you review your business plan at least once a year, and update it as your business continues to grow and change.

If you are planning to seek financing at any time in the formation or future of your business, you cannot begin the process without a well-thought-out business plan. If you don't know how to write one; learn. Here is a basic outline of a start-up business plan. Make sure yours includes each of these points.

Executive Summary – A concise summary of your company. This should grab the attention of anyone who might consider investing in your company and will be a guideline to get you through the rest of the organizational process of your business plan.

Mission – describe the ultimate goal of your business, or create your own mission statement

Company – Describe what your business does, when the company was formed/founded (date), your company organization (Sole Proprietor, LLC, etc.) and where your offices will be located.

The Business – Describe your product or service. Is it in the "start-up," "building," "growth" stage? Discuss your income goals by month and year (usually stated pre-tax or gross), and identify at what time (year) you plan to achieve the next level in sales growth. Describe why you feel this is an attainable goal. This is key information when seeking financing, so be sure to provide lots of detail here.

Product or Service – This is where you will detail exactly what your products and/or services are.

The Market – Describe what or who your target market is, detail who your clients will be, how and where you will find them, whether or not they are buying your product or service from someone else currently, and how you will market yourself so that these clients will buy from you instead of your competition.

Competition – Discuss and detail who your competitors are and what your product/service will do to create a competitive edge that will drive these clients to you.

Risks – Describe what risks you may have as they relate to the product/service you are selling, how you can overcome these risks, and what you can do to dominate your market.

Management – If you will be working with other teams to achieve your goals, outline it here.

Capital – If you require outside funding, detail how much you need, what it will be used for, how your profits will help you repay the debt, and in what period of time.

Financial Plan – Detail all your income, assets, holdings, anything that will give an investor a clear picture of where you are today, and what, if any, collateral is available to secure the loan.

Sales Summary – Current sales, past sales, and proposed future sales.

Balance Sheet – Listing of assets and liabilities, for last year, this year, and proposed future years. (This may be available from your CPA, or in your financial software, like QuickBooks.)

Goals – This is where you detail or forecast where you see your business growing over the next 5-10 years. You can discuss growth as it pertains to adding staff or subcontractors, additional equipment or education, and industry organizations that you will be involved with to help keep your industry strong and growing.

Although we know there are many successful and thriving VA practices that do not have a business plan in place, we do encourage you to take the time to put together this important piece of information about your plans and goals, even if it's just for you. And go back every year and update it based on everything you've learned about your business and the industry during the past year. It should always be a work in progress.

As you start, you may not need, nor be able to provide information for all of these areas, but do the best you can. Set up a basic plan that includes all the areas that pertain to you now, and make any necessary adjustments in the future. If you are seeking private or SBA funding initially, check with your local financial institution, or SBA approved loan processor to make sure you have the format needed to secure such funding.

If you need help, often your CPA and/or corporate attorney can provide you with information about reputable places that will help you design and implement a good business plan.

Contracts and Forms

Depending on your specialty, you may need any number of basic forms to get started. Initially, you will need some sort of "Work for Hire Agreement"—something that explains your relationship with every client you are to do business with, and a Time Record of some sort to keep track of the time utilized on client projects. Some people use online time management tools, such as TraxTime, and TimeSlips, but basic handwritten forms can be easily created and used during the start-up phase of your business.

Additional technologies such as, FreshBooks (an invoicing and time-tracking online software option), and project management software such as Basecamp and Central Desktop also provide options for tracking your time and managing client projects.

Do not start your business off on the wrong foot—make sure that each and every client, even if they are your brother or sister, signs an Agreement with you so that they have a clear picture of your relationship, expectations, and how you do business. Please see the back of this book for samples or resources to contracts and forms.

If you specialize in any particular area, you may need additional contracts and forms, such as: Retainer Agreement – for potential clients who will pay you up-front; Resume writing—you'll need a resume questionnaire; Legal pleadings— you will need a form detailing how each particular pleading is formatted; telephone contact sheets—if you make calls, you will need some way of recapping for the client who you contacted, when, and the call results; and many other such forms will be necessary depending on the main focus of your business.

You can create these forms on your own; detailing your specific informational needs, or search online for additional resources. Many times industry organizations like IVAA.org will provide you a forms library as a benefit of your membership. Or, you can find business chat areas where people may

Record Keeping

Accurate record keeping is vital to the success of your business. You must keep track of every hour you work, even if it's volunteer, or "free" hours offered to new customers, as well as having receipts for business equipment and supplies, meeting and membership costs, postage or printing, and advertising. Software such as QuickBooks provides an easy to use program that allows you to categorize expenses and income so that when it's time to file your taxes, all the information is organized and easy to use for you or your CPA.

Don't forget to keep track of your business mileage to the post office, office supply store, client meeting, or business trip. These are all tax deductible. Check with a qualified CPA to find out what records are needed, and what items are tax deductible.

You will also need to keep track of your administrative time. This includes the time used to invoice clients, order office supplies, research potential clients, build client databases, set up and implement advertising and marketing programs, etc. All of this time needs to be tracked and documented to assist you in capturing this time when setting your fees. This is time used to handle the administrative functions of your business and should be included as a cost of doing business. You must find the time to do these tasks, which will take away from your billable hours. Don't forget to include them when considering expenses that will need to be added to your base hourly rate.

Delegating Business Tasks

You've heard a lot about CPAs and attorneys in this chapter. It's important that you hire experts to make sure you are running your businesses properly, legally, and taking full advantage of any tax benefits owning a business provides. This is money well-spent.

Just as you will be educating potential clients on the benefits of using your expertise to accomplish the tasks for which you are the professional, take your own advice and hire professionals to make sure your business will continue to grow and prosper. Even start-ups have a CPA, attorney, and insurance agent.

Just as your potential clients will interview you, interview these professionals you will be hiring, too. The best way is to do some networking and either meet qualified professionals or get referrals from other businesspeople you trust. These people will be partners in your business, independent contractors who should want to know what your needs are, what your business is all about, and how they can help you be successful. These are the same qualifications our potential clients will be looking for from us.

Initially, if money is tight, you may also consider a barter agreement with these independent contractors. They may have needs you could fulfill in exchange for their services. Be sure that you have a clear understanding of how the barter relationship will work, and keep track of all hours you are writing off, and request the same from them.

The Executive Summary

The items in this chapter will take a while to execute. Don't get overwhelmed; just take one task at a time. If you skip one now, it may come back to haunt you in the future. Make sure all your ducks are in a row. Know how many hours a week you will devote to your VA practice, which equipment you need to buy, write your business plan, and hire the necessary professionals to set up your business. You can't go this one alone; you are going to need to get some help. The expert advice will be worth the cost and it will provide you with peace of mind.

Once you have all these items checked off your "to-do" list, you will be ready to move on to the more "fun" aspects of starting your own business that you'll read about in the next few chapters, like naming your business, marketing yourself and setting your rates. The material covered in this chapter is all the housekeeping you need to start your business properly. The hard work you do now will pay off with a successful and profitable business for many years to come.

Start-Up Options At-A-Glance

Item	Wish List	Bare Bones
Desktop computer & monitor	$1,000	$650
Color Inkjet	$500 (top of the line)	$100 (entry level)
Laser Printer (if needed)	$500 (color)	$150 (black and white)
Fax Machine	$150	$25-$50 for computer software

Fax Service	$35/mth - 2nd phone line	free via email
Scanner	$400 (top of the line)	$100 (entry level)
Business Phone	~$50/month (land line)	$25/month (cable VOIP phone)
Small Copier	$300	---
Broadband Internet	$60/month	$30/month
Office Rent	$600/month and up	$0 or additional tax write-off
Software		
MS Office (if needed)	$499 (2010 Professional)	n/a (included with most computers)
Money management	$230 (2011 Quickbooks Pro)	$90 (Microsoft Money Sm. Biz)
Office Supplies	$100	$100
Answering Machine	$8/month for voicemail	$20 and up for machine
Calculator	$10 and up	Free (online @calculator.com)
Website Hosting	$10/month and up	$4/month and up
Scheduling Options		
Calendar	$10 and up	free in Outlook
Planner/Appt. book	$10 and up	free in Outlook
Marketing Materials (*)		
Brochures (100)	$100	$73.50 (color inkjet) $165.00 (color laserjet)
Letterhead (500)	$100	$120 (color inkjet)
Business Cards (500)	$40 and up	$32.80 from your inkjet on specialty business card paper
Professional Memberships		
VA Group (IVAA)	$137/1st year,	$137
Local Chambers	$50-$300 each (varies)	$50-$300 (varies)

*all costs are approximated, based on specialty paper that may be purchased through resources like tigerdirect.com – prices will vary based on your pattern selection. In some cases, it is less expensive to have your marketing materials professionally printed than it is to print them yourself.

Chapter Links and Resources

Freelance Project Work Resources	www.elance.com
	www.guru.com
	www.oDesk.com
Transcription Options	www.sten-tel.com
	www.startstop.com
	www.transcriptiongear.com
	www.mtdaily.com
	www.nch.com.au/scribe/
Copies	www.FedExKinkos.com
	www.OfficeMax.com
Accounting Software	www.intuit.com
	www.peachtree.com
Time Tracking Software	www.spudcity.com/traxtime/index.html
	www.timeslips.com
	www.syntap.com
Invoicing/Time Tracking	www.freshbooks.com
Project management software	www.basecamp.com
	www.centraldesktop.com
	www.myclientspot.com
Online Faxing/Phone options	www.eFax.com
	www.ringcentral.com
	www.freedomvoice.com
	www.myfax.com
Industry Associations	www.ivaa.org
Legal forms and documents	www.nolo.com

Chapter Three

Branding

For just a moment, imagine tasting your favorite soft drink. Now recall the name of it, now the tagline, now the jingle, now the logo. All those aspects define the brand of an item. It creates an identifiable impression on the public's mind. You want to do the same thing (albeit on a smaller scale) for your business.

Branding has recently become an all encompassing catch phrase to identify a strategy that 'brands' you, your company, and your products or services, and helps us to understand the impact and results that finding and establishing a brand can do to advance your exposure, recognition, and success.

As branding has continued to evolve in the corporate world, and especially in small and home-based businesses, it also encompasses your personal brand, who you are, what you stand for, your business practices and ethics, too. While your clients are doing business with your company, it still comes down to them knowing, liking, and trusting you, which all links back to your reputation. These elements should also be an integral part of your brand elements.

Naming Your Business

What to name your business is a big decision—it is a very important part of the process of forming your business. First, do some research to get a frame of reference. Check your local Yellow Pages under a few main listing categories, like, "Secretarial Services," or "Transcription," or any other specialty that might be your niche. See what names you like and which you don't. Now you will have a general idea of the type of name you want your business to have, and those you do not want to emulate.

Here are a few things to consider when naming your business:

- Incorporate the word "Virtual" into the company name to identify your business focus.
- Come up with a company name with the first letter toward the beginning of the alphabet. Then you'll be listed near the top in the

Yellow Pages or in association or organizational directories. People who are letting their "fingers do the walking" many times will start at the top of the category.

- Use something fun that may help people remember you, and your product or service more easily....for example—"Stat Medical Transcribers" This name identifies their specialty of Medical Transcription, and says they work "fast."

- Most importantly, check the "business listing section" of your White Pages Directory, and do some in-depth research online to make sure that you are not choosing a company name that someone in this or another industry is currently using.

You want to be certain that you are not using a company name that someone in another industry may have thought of first. This could put you in a legal battle with them to find out who 'registered' the use of that name, first. If it so happens you didn't, this could cost you thousands in attorney fees, and in changing and re-marketing your new business name.

If you change your mind about your business name down the road, prepare to spend quite a bit for that change. You'll need new business cards, letterhead, brochures, association and organizational listings, websites, logos, and possibly telephone numbers, e-mail accounts, fax numbers, etc. It becomes a daunting and expensive task. That's why it's important to invest the time and research into picking a business name that can be with you for the long term.

Come up with several possibilities. Bounce your ideas off your friends and colleagues. Ask what they do and don't like about names you suggest. Together, you may be able to come up with a new name that is a better fit for you.

The most important thing in naming your business is to be sure it's something that represents who you are, helps clients understand what you do and how you work, that you are a professional entrepreneur, is memorable and/or fun, and is something that you can live with for the long term.

Tag Lines

Tag lines are short, one sentence business statements that sum up exactly what it is you do for clients. We see tag lines all day long, like McDonald's latest, "I'm lovin' it®," or something like the old Alka Seltzer ads, "Plop...plop...fizz...fizz...oh, what a relief it is!" Tag lines are something that you want everyone to remember, because if they remember your tag line, they'll remember you when they need your product or service.

You will want to bounce your tag line off of friends and colleagues, and you may want to update it as time goes on and your business evolves. It should be memorable to everyone you tell it to, so that they can better understand your product/service and can refer business to you. You should also incorporate it into the end of your 30-second infomercials which will be discussed in the next section.

For example, consider this tagline: "Your business support specialist." What does that mean? Do you provide IT support, administrative support, supplies, consulting? It's not specific enough. What about, "Your Admin Problem Solver?" A little better, but still not memorable enough. You will probably go through several reworks. Come up with a tag line and try it on for size. Ask colleagues for suggestions. Overall, this final statement should address to prospective clients, "What's in it for me?" What will they gain by having done business with you....what problem will you solve for them...what need will you fulfill?

Try to come up with something catchy, and don't be afraid to use parts of famous tag lines like, "Nike, just do it" —just make certain that you do not use it exactly as they have presented it which would be copyright infringement. Be creative, and have fun with it. The more catchy your tag line, the easier it will be for people to remember it, and in turn, remember you, and your product or service. One of my favorites is from a Chiropractor friend, "We gently crack your aching back!"—this tells you exactly what her business is, in a fun, concise way.

Take your time developing your tag line, and revise it until you feel you have finally come up with something that says it all. You'll be amazed at how easily people will remember you by remembering your tag line.

30-Second Commercials

Many organizations and leads groups allow you a 30 or 60-second infomercial that tells people, in a short period of time, exactly what it is you do, and how you could help them with your product or service. Some may call it your "elevator speech"—a short explanation you'd give to someone in the time it takes to arrive at your destination in an elevator if they asked what you do for a living.

This should not be a laundry list of your services, but more of a short story that tells people how you can help them, how you have helped someone else, or solved a problem or issue that makes their business run more smoothly.

Play around with this and time yourself to be sure that you can fit it into the allowed 30 or 60-seconds, and then practice it in front of the mirror until you have it memorized and it flows smoothly. Remember to "smile"; people are more likely to positively respond to you if you're smiling. Even if you're setting up your voicemail message, a smile translates very well verbally. You will be amazed at how many people will say that you're so upbeat, or sound so happy all the time…it's simply because you're always smiling, even over the phone.

Your infomercial will probably never be delivered the same way twice; unless you find something that fits exactly, then you'll probably have no problem in memorizing it and using it all the time. Be wary of being too monotone or projecting that your message is "memorized." People will find you insincere, and it will be quite obvious that you're just quoting a script you've written for yourself. That's why it's probably best to change it up occasionally, but keep your "tag line," discussed in the previous section, as that is the one thing you'll want to quote exactly.

Communicate what's in it for the client, what problem will you solve, what makes you different from their in-house staff, or temps. What is it about you that makes you excel in the services you are offering? Do you have certifications, many years of experience, or the highest level of professionalism and expertise that they won't find in their current staff?

Working with "virtual" businesses is more of a partnership than it is like being an employee. We are business owners, just like they are, and have a much better understanding of what it takes to run and operate a successful business. So communicate the advantages of using "virtual" services, and educate them on the industry and how virtual businesses are working together to make their clients more profitable and productive. In essence, what we're selling is time, and allowing them the opportunity to have highly skilled support, without the expenses associated with an in-house employee. We're freeing up their time, or that of another staff person, to be able to work on other income-generating projects.

Having a well polished 30 or 60-second infomercial will go far in helping your business and the VA industry grow. Take the time to develop it and test variations on a regular basis. Friends and colleagues will be very helpful in designing and implementing your infomercial.

Creating a Website

Working "virtually" demands that you have an Internet presence. You MUST have a website, or you will not be taken seriously. Even if you're just looking for local business, a website is a great place to market your products or services, and a great place to create your web-based "brochure."

Although it should not completely mirror your print brochure version, your website should cover many of the same things that your brochure will.

On the Home Page, we suggest some of that classy "infomercial" verbiage to give surfers a quick glance at what you do, and how you could serve them.

Website Guidelines

Minimally, your website should have three to five pages. In addition to a Home Page, you may include any combination of the following topic pages:

- About us—About your company, how it was formed, and past experience that makes you an expert in this field. Your photo and something about you personally is suggested because of the 'virtual' nature of our business. Prospects will be more comfortable considering you if they feel there's a real person behind the business.

- Products/Services—This is the page to list your specialties. Be specific, but not too wordy. You want basic information where someone can quickly see if you fit their need.

- Links/Resources—This may be where you list your certifications or memberships in industry associations, and/or resources that may be of interest to someone who is doing business with you.

- Contact Us—A simple list of how to reach you, or a form to submit a question or get a quote on a proposed project.

- Sample Work—With permission from your clients, you may want to provide some samples of work you have completed. This is especially important for a VA who specializes in graphic design, or web development. This will help potential clients experience your talents.

- Testimonials—A must on anyone's website. If you're trying to keep costs down and minimize your number of pages, or just starting out and don't have any testimonials yet, consider mingling them among the other pages on your website, or have a Testimonials page and spread a few of them out over the other pages, too. One good way to make a hit with your clients and drive more traffic to your site is to offer clients a "link" to their site from the testimonial you'll be posting to your site. It's a great way to honor your current clients, help them get more traffic at their websites, and communicate your entrepreneurial spirit to prospective clients browsing your site.

You may want to consider additional pages...."in the news," articles you've written, or articles written about you, or a "newsletter." Any of these pages would be a great way to get people to re-visit your site when looking for fresh content, and provide them with more information about what you do. Another page could be a Frequently Asked Questions, or "FAQ" page, which explains to potential clients how to work with you and what some of your company guidelines are.

> *"A website is tremendously important to business success. The website is the portal to our company. We keep its search engine optimized and market it in every phase of our presentations. We receive a lot of referrals from the site and update it continuously so clients will visit often."*
> Caroline Wright,
> The Wright Solution

Do a Google search for VAs, and check out some of the many ways that you can represent yourself. Do not, however, copy anyone else's content or site layout. Instead, research other VA websites to help narrow down what you would like on your own.

Rates: To List or Not to List?

What about a "rates" page? Should you have one or not? There are two schools of thought on that issue and you need to decide for yourself whether or not to list your prices. Opponents of listing your rates on your site argue that it is not the best way to communicate to prospective clients, and it may just give your rates away to unethical people who would take your pricing and undercut it if they know they're up against you in bidding on a project, or if marketing to the same niche as you.

Listing rates also encourages "price shoppers"; those who just want to find the 'cheapest' VA. These people do not care about the quality of the work, and will most likely be the type of client who will continually deduct from your invoice or constantly be re-negotiating your price based on their perception of the value of your work. You may find that they want to control all aspects of your relationship. This could be a dangerous threat to the growth and perception of your company. The one time you decide NOT to give in to their demands for a lower price or invoice reduction may result in them speaking badly of you to others. Just not a position you would want to put yourself in.

Another caution about posting your rates on your website: it's often better to discuss with the prospective client the rates on an individual basis. You may decide that it makes more sense to base your rate on the actual project or the level of expertise required to complete a particular task than a one-size-fits-all flat rate for every project and every client. While you may charge an

Branding 45

hourly rate for most of your services, some clients may prefer a project quote so they know the maximum total bill they'll owe you, and this would require a custom quote. Other services may make more sense to know what the "per each" price is, for example per database entry, per word for transcription, per website page, etc. To account for all the possibilities in rates, variations, and different projects, if listing them on your website could confuse your reader and not allow you any flexibility in quoting your rates if you anticipate a project being more time-consuming or difficult than most others in that category, it may be best not to post pricing at your site.

Despite the possible drawbacks you could experience in listing your prices, many VAs choose to list them, or at least a range for their services. Why? For one, advertising your rates automatically weeds out people that won't pay professional rates for VA services. It also communicates to the client that you are confident in your pricing structure and have nothing to hide from your clients.

> "One of the things I found out early is if you set your rates too low, you end up with people who haggle over every nickel, and those are often the most difficult to work with. I asked myself: will the work I generate from these customers pay to cover my doctor bills while I try and cure my ulcer?"
>
> Nina Feldman,
> Nina Feldman Connections

However, in some cases, speaking directly to the potential client about your rates, and the level of service and expertise they will be getting, can quash a professional prospect's concerns and help educate them on the advantages of working with you, the level of experience you bring to the table and why it's necessary to charge the rates that you do. This also allows you the opportunity to quote a project in a more pleasing manner. A great sales technique is to quote a 'per each' price, which may be easier to accept than quoting them an entire project dollar amount. By handling pricing concerns on an individual basis, you get the opportunity to get a feel for the best way to quote this client. If pricing seems to be their 'hot button', a 'per each' price gives them a better way to understand the total cost, by considering the return they'll receive by looking at a 'per piece' cost.

Over the past several years there is has been a trend to offer packages and programs (in lieu of retainers) to help prospects grasp what can be accomplished in a certain period of time. If you happen to offer bookkeeping services, a package might include the client's monthly invoicing, paying bills, checkbook input and balancing statements, and managing monthly expenses. You could figure what the normal time would be to accomplish these tasks, multiply by your hourly rate and give them a total dollar amount they could budget for each month.

Another example might be for someone who handles article marketing for a client. Your package or program could include so many articles posted each month to so many free article sites, as well as to an established blog and promotion on social media – add up the hours required, multiply by your hourly rate, and post this package/program price on your site.

> "I did a survey of local bookkeeping businesses and put my rate around the middle to higher end. I also took into consideration how many billable hours I wanted to work and how much I wanted to make."
> Kimberley Thomas-Catanzaro, Bookkeeping & Secretarial Services

In this way, the client isn't just considering that hourly rate, not understanding what could be accomplished in that time, which makes it much easier for them to understand the value and benefit of working with you.

To list or not list your rates is an individual decision. Consider the pros and cons of each option. You can always change your mind down the road, no matter what your initial decision is.

Getting Set Up on the World Wide Web

Now that you have the basics outlined for your company website, there are many ways to actually get it set up on the World Wide Web. Obviously, if you're a web designer, this process will be a breeze. For those of you who may be somewhat technologically challenged, you will have to go through this process.

1) Create and look into the availability of your domain name (www.myvirtualbusiness.com)—keep in mind that you want something that will be easy for people to remember when they're trying to find you, and also something that represents your business, much like the process of naming your business. Once you have identified the domain name you'd like to consider, you must find out if someone else already has that domain. Your best option is to check with someone who can register your domain, like a web host. Since you will also need a web host, unless you have your own servers, you can enter the domain name at www.namecheap.com, or www.tigertech.net, just to name a few. Once you have found a domain name that no one has already registered, register it immediately before someone else does.

2) Decide on your web host by checking out some of the many reasonably priced web hosts outlined at the end of this Chapter. You can also get "free" website hosting through ISP's like AOL and Yahoo and companies like Vistaprint, but we do not suggest these for a

BRANDING 47

professional business website. These free or extremely inexpensive offerings usually mean you will have a very long and hard to identify URL. You may also be required to have annoying banner or popup ads, and other less than professional features on your website. Since you want your business to be represented in the best light possible, avoid using these types of hosts for your VA business site. You may also be eligible for free hosting services through association memberships. The International Virtual Assistants Association (www.ivaa.org) offers free website hosting as a part of their membership benefits.

3) Hire an expert to set up and upload the pages. Once you have all the content, information, logo, and other information together, you need to get your website set up. If you're not a web designer, you need to find someone who is. Look at industry organization sites, find a site you really like and contact that person to see who they used, or ask someone you know for a referral. You want someone who has good skills, but will not set your site up where they have their own specific "code." Many website designers have their own proprietary code, which is great, until something happens and you do not want to use this person to update your website any longer. Using their own "proprietary" code will prevent anyone else from being able to come in afterwards and make any changes or updates. Make sure that you have a detailed contract that addresses these issues so that you won't have problems in the future.

4) Setup meta tags and keywords. Your web design expert will be handling all your meta tags and keywords, but you will be the best person to provide the list of keywords that will be most appropriate for your business. Make a list of words that you believe your prospective clients might enter into a search engine, like Google, to find someone that provides the products/services that you do. The more keywords you can come up with, the easier it will be for people to find you, and the higher your rankings will be at the search engines.

5) As your budget allows, work with organizations that can setup your new website with all of the main search engines. Once your website has been accepted by the top search engines, get in the habit of regularly resubmitting your site to bring it back to the top of the search engine lists.

6) Change your website content consistently. Every time you change the content of your website, your site will spider out this new content and all of the search engines will pick your site up again, as something

new to resource on the Internet. This is a great way to re-establish top rankings with major search engines on a continual basis. We suggest changing something at your website at least once every six months, but if possible, once a quarter.

7) Once your site is ready to go live, view it in a variety of browsers, like AOL, Yahoo, Firefox, Internet Explorer, etc. They all work a little differently and you want to be sure that your website translates effectively in all major browsers.

In recent years, the boom in the area of blogs has presented us with an additional website platform option. Because blogs are an 'open source', search engines look favorably upon this option, and because of the ease of use and ability to make updates/changes daily, a blog platform can easily be used to create a website that is attractive and professional at a far lower cost to maintain.

We still suggest that you host the blog (our favorite is wordpress.org) and if you decide to have one in addition to your static website, it's always best to optimize both by using a URL such as www.mystaticwebsite.com/blog as your blog URL.

Using a blog platform for your website does provide many advantages, as well as a few disadvantages. One is that it's difficult to disguise that you're using a blog platform – in some cases, depending upon your target or ideal client, this may be looked upon as you being a 'cheaper' alternative, or less professional. The sidebars on either side of your theme are present on every page, so you'll need to plan these areas wisely.

You will also want to consider your storage needs. A static website can hold much larger files than a blog is able to do, so if you will need to host or store larger files, this may not be the best option for your needs.

Check with others who use both a blog platform and static website to help you determine which will be your best option.

Your website will be part of your business image and it needs to reflect your professionalism. Do not use lots of different fonts or inappropriate photos and personal images. Although it might be nice to mention a "personal" or "family" web page and put a link at your company site, we suggest that you keep business and personal separate. This should represent your company only, and be as professional as possible.

Your website IS your FIRST IMPRESSION to potential clients. Make sure it has the look and feel that you want. Even for "virtual" clients who initiate contact with you by phone, your website can be your portal to educate people about how business savvy you are, and provide them with a way to "immediately" find out about you, your clients, and whether or not you will be the best option to fulfill their needs.

Signature Lines

A well crafted signature line can be an incredibly valuable tool in your marketing arsenal. You can include everything from your favorite quote by Thomas Edison, to a quick link to your website 'free tips and tricks' articles or newsletter. Use your signature line to brand yourself, and communicate features and benefits in a brief, concise way that makes the reader crave more information. Don't make it into a manifesto, but you can find ways to bring attention to yourself and your market segment through your signature line.

Consider multiple signature lines for use in different arenas, and be cautious of participation guidelines by associations, listservs and online groups that may limit the number of lines, size, or content of your signature lines.

Here are just a few considerations for inclusion in a signature line that will help educate potential and current clients, peers, and colleagues that will help increase your exposure to referrals and business growth:

- Website URL
- Tagline
- Newsletter sign-up
- Tips or articles sign-up or links to your site
- Certification designations
- Phone, fax, e-mail contact data
- Branding items – company name, logos
- Brief list of benefits of working with you
- List of new services being offered
- Link to your blog
- Link to connect with you on social media
- Tout your membership in an industry association
- Announce upcoming seminars, conferences or trainings

Taking a little time to create and implement multiple signature lines will help to drive traffic to your website, or entice clients to take 'action' and connect with you on some professional level that can help you increase your client base, or expand the types of services your current clients utilize. Adding a professional signature line to your marketing tool belt is an easy and inexpensive way to bring attention to you and your practice.

Setting Your Fees

Okay, how many of you browsed the Table of Contents and jumped right to this Section of Chapter Three? It is, by far, the most challenging part of getting your business started. The "Virtual Business" industry is still in its infancy, and because the scope of services provided can range from answering e-mails to redesigning a website, your fee base can be quite simple, or extremely complex.

> "During the 3-year transition from part-time to full-time, I didn't increase my rates at all which was a big mistake. This was mainly a confidence problem, worrying that if I increased my rates I would lose clients. In my first two-years as a full-time VA, I have since developed a policy of increasing rates every other year."
> Caroline Wright, The Wright Solution

The best way to decide where to start is by first deciding on a few basic things. What is your income goal, and how many hours per week will you have to do client projects? For example, let's say that your target income is $50,000 per year, and you would like to work a minimum of 30-billable hours per week. You would take $50,000, divide it by 12 (months), then that figure by four (weeks), and then by 30 (billable hours per week). The solution to that problem is: $34.72. That means that your hourly rate would have to be about $35/hour to reach your target income.

But that's not all that you need to take into consideration. Now you need to add your expenses....all of your expenses. You must add overhead into that figure. Your overhead includes things like: renting office space, electricity, telephone service, fax line, Internet service, web hosting, marketing, invoicing clients, bookkeeping, professional services, office supplies, software updates, equipment repairs and replacement, etc. Once you have attached an annual dollar figure to all of those overhead costs, divide it by 12, then four, then 30, as above, to see how much, per hour, needs to be added to that $35 per hour rate, in order to cover all those expenses. Don't forget to include what you'll be paying an accountant, attorney, professional printer (for letterhead, business cards, brochures, etc.) into the mix. This will give you the most realistic idea of what base your hourly rate should be for most projects.

Again, this is just your base hourly rate. In addition to all of this, you will also want to add something in for your profit margin. These profits will be the monies you are able to set aside to expand and grow your business. If you decide to specialize or change your specialization, these profits will be what you use to keep your business running when business is soft, or if something catastrophic happens, like you're hospitalized for a period of time and unable to work. You must try and cover your expenses under any unforeseen circumstances.

Now that you have finalized your hourly rate, it's time to consider your expertise and the industry you serve. You must research your industry and find out what the average rate is for others that provide similar services. Take into consideration if you're using more specialized software like Adobe Illustrator or Photoshop, to complete client tasks. These software programs are very expensive, as are their upgrades, and they may require additional training to gain the expertise needed to complete the task for the client. All of these things should be considered when setting your rates.

> *"My basic approach on pricing was to use a flat rate. The client is buying my time and the cost is the same whether I am writing your business plan or stuffing envelopes."*
> Caroline Wright,
> The Wright Solution

You will also want to consider all "outside" client expenses as separate line items on your invoices with a particular percentage added to the actual costs for providing this service to your clients. These might include the cost to print a client project, or specific office supplies needed to do a client task. You will also want to show these as separate invoice line items so that you can create more accurate reports detailing your actual business costs, and client project costs, as well as, finding out which product or service you provide that may be more or less profitable. This will help your business evolve into something that is most profitable to your skill set. See the section on Record Keeping in Chapter Two for more information on how to setup your basic accounting system.

VAs who charge lower rates tend to get the lower end clients. The clients who really value your expertise and understand the value of working with a VA will have no problem in paying rates that match your level of skill and expertise. If your rates are too low, you won't be able to take on enough work to stay profitable, and this doesn't help you or your clients. If you go out of business, they have to find and TRAIN someone else to do what you've been doing for them. If you want your business to be successful and you want to be in business for many years to come, you need to be realistic about charging reasonable and profitable rates. Starting off too low simply communicates to prospective clients that you don't think you're worth it. You will only attract those clients who are looking for something for nothing, and do not understand the value of having skilled, experienced support, without the overhead or training involved in on-site employees or temps.

Charging reasonable rates aligned with others within your industry is the best way to establish and grow a healthy business. With a little bit of research, and some time to consider all that's needed to run a business, you'll easily be able to set rates you and your clients can live with, and help you keep your business running smoothly for many years to come.

You should also increase your prices yearly, or bi-annually. Your costs to do business will always increase along with the normal "cost of living" – which averages three percent per year. Don't be concerned with losing any clients, research tells us this is very minimal, and the increase in your hourly rates will usually cover any business you may lose as a result of an increase. The clients that will stop doing business with you because you raise your prices a few dollars an hour are really not the "Type A" clients who are going to help your business grow.

> *"I did not increase my rates for the first four years in business, which was a mistake. You have to be confident that you deserve your rate increases, and know what expenses you have that increase every year. Now I increase my rates every year at the first of the year."*
> Janice Wlodarski, Progressive Publishing Services

Setting "A" Client Criteria

When you're first getting started, setting "A client" criteria seems like wasted time. You'll certainly be tempted to take on any business that comes your way, even some that you may not be qualified to handle, because you believe that if you don't take everything, you won't be in business for long. If you are not qualified or have the needed skills to complete a project, do yourself a favor, either refer that potential client to someone you know who has the necessary skills or pass on the business altogether. You will do nothing but hurt your reputation by trying to be the "expert" at some task you are unfamiliar with. You could also consider working with other VAs who have the needed skills on a sub-contractor basis, or setup a mutually beneficial "finder's fee" that will help you, the sub-contractor, and the client.

If you plan your business as suggested in Chapter One, you will have some resources to keep you afloat until you become more established. Trying to be all things to all people simply makes you a master of nothing. Not everyone is meant to be a generalist and provide a wide range of services to a wide market of potential clients. If being a generalist doesn't fit with your skill set, take the leap to provide specialized services in a specific, niche market. You may even find specializing will make your business more profitable and grow more quickly because you're differentiating yourself from your competition.

Although you may need to provide a range of services initially to find your niche, decide which projects give you the most satisfaction. What industry are you providing this particular service for? Do you enjoy working with people in that industry? Do you have reasonable access and information to successfully market to this industry?

Deciding on your specialty will help you in detailing your client criteria. Once you know what products and services they need, you can outline what software, equipment and additional training you may need to serve that particular industry. This information will also help you decide your rates. Once you have that outlined, then you can start to envision what the perfect client will look like, and this is where your client criteria is born.

For example, if you specialize in Realtor support, you may find that your client criteria fall into several categories. "A" clients are independent real estate professionals selling a minimum of $7-10 million dollars per year; "B" clients are independent real estate professionals selling a minimum of $1-7 million dollars per year; and "C" clients are real estate professionals who are newer to the industry and are still doing many of the tasks you specialize in and are just not yet ready to take the plunge. The final client category may be "mixed" clients, those who are not in the real estate industry, but who need some of the services you provide. Although you may not spend any of your marketing budget trying to find those "C" or "Mixed" clients, you will still get some by referral, or because they are just checking to see what it might "cost" them to have a professional upload their new listings to their three websites, instead of doing it at 3:00 a.m. themselves! It is also wise not to put all your eggs into one industry. As with our Realtor support example, there are slow periods in the real estate market which translates to less business for you to support. You will want some 'Mixed" clients in your client list to help supplement your income during these slower times in your niche. Learning to recognize the difference in these client categories will go far in helping you decide who you should and should not be doing business with.

> "I usually set up an initial phone call to discuss their needs and from there I can determine if I am the best person to assist them and also if there is a connection. If I am not, I either recommend another VA or have them visit the IVAA site to complete and RFP."
>
> Linda Siniscal,
> Third Hand Secretarial™

Now that you know what your client categories are, establish where you will find the two client types that are at the top of your criteria, and how you will best market to them. Research where these potential clients "hang out." Ask your current clientele who fit into your top categories—the ones that have the income to support virtual services, and who are making an income that allows them to understand the value of their own time, and realize that doing tasks not directly related to their income is not only unprofitable, but counter-productive—where they hang out on the Web, and what industry magazines or periodicals they subscribe to. You can also do an online search for relevant industry organizations and associations those types of clients would belong to. Look for list-serves, social media groups and chats that they may participate in and find ways to market to them effectively through these resources.

> "I make my decisions based on the phone call or other inquiry, and have developed a feel for whether or not the client is a good match. I automatically disqualify anyone who wants to haggle on fees or who raises any of a number of red flags that you develop intuitively (too big a rush, wishy washy, etc.)."
> Katie Baird, Loose Ends

Identifying your client criteria can help you bring the crème to the top. To be a strong and profitable company you need to work with the best clients possible. When setting your criteria, be sure and consider the way they do business with you. For example, do they pay on time, do they try to get you to reduce your pricing, do they provide you with referrals, or do they have poor communication skills which cause problems with you having to rework projects that weren't properly communicated? These all make a huge impact on your ability to serve them well, and keep doing business with them at a reasonable price. Doing business with just anyone can be a disservice to you and your reputation. If you try to be all things to all people, they will expect that, and more!

By charging higher rates you will find that you will attract better clients, have fewer client issues, and be able to build a more profitable business booking less hours with fewer clients, leaving time open for you to continue to develop, market and grow your business.

Tracking Client Time and Time Management

Few components to a VAs practice are more important than time. You will need to manage your own time, determine the time you have available for client projects, and your actual "time on task" spent on client projects. Before you can manage your client's time, you need to manage your own.

As you begin, you may feel you have nothing but time on your hands, but this is the BEST time to put good time management systems in place that will help you in all levels of your business.

The simplest time management system is a "to do" list. Whether you keep a separate legal pad with your list, or enter it daily into your online or hard copy calendar, a "to do" list will help you stay focused on what you need to do and allows you the ability to track your accomplishments and results. Don't forget to include a section that indicates when the project MUST be completed so that you stay on top of your most critical deadlines.

Check off and add tasks to your list throughout the day. At the end of the day, transfer the tasks left on the old list, and re-enter them on to a new list, or just keep the information handy so you can continue to work on these unfinished tasks in the days to come.

> *"My client criteria is specific – the work must be within my knowledge/experience base and must be family friendly."*
> Judy Vorfeld,
> Office Support Services

Online systems provide you with the ability to set reminders that will help you stay on top of the tasks you need to accomplish and the time in which you need them completed. There is no one "right" system. How do you prefer to work? Do you like to have everything on your computer, or do you like having a physical notebook or calendar (like Franklin Covey or Day Timer) type to-do list? Work within the system that makes the most sense for you. The most important thing is to plan your day. If you don't, you are "planning to fail!"

As outlined in a previous Chapter, there are also project management software options online such as Basecamp, Central Desktop and MyClientSpot. Some of them even offer 'free' versions that may be beneficial during your initial growth stages.

Your next step is to find the best way to manage how much time you have available for client work. Go back to the notes you made about setting your fees. Make a note of the total number of hours you decided you would have available to work on client projects. Use that figure, along with your current client commitments, to decide how best to accomplish current client projects, and stay on schedule to complete them in the time allotted. This is an important part of running an ethical business—you must do what you promised when you said you would! As projects come in throughout the week, add them to your client project management sheet, or calendar, to keep on track of your deadlines and your ability to take on and set deadlines for future projects. If you have retainer clients, be sure and figure in their "proposed" weekly project commitments so that you have the time available that they have already committed to and paid for.

If you're working with sub-contractors, be sure to take note of when they are to have the completed project back to you, and allow enough time for you to check their work and forward the project to the client within the agreed upon deadline. This type of work, and the available time of your subcontractors needs to be monitored and added to the time, you personally, will have available for client projects. Not monitoring this process could be deadly to your reputation and overall business health.

Finally, how will you track your time on task, or billable time, for your client projects? You can set up something as simple as a Daily Time Record, which provides the client name, project date, details of the project, quantity done, start time, stop time, kind of work, and billable time. This allows you to keep track of each individual project and the time it takes to complete it. This information will also help when trying to bid on future projects for the same type of work. Other options to track client project times include software programs designed for this specific task. Systems such as TraxTime, TimeSlips, and Freshbooks are some of the more popular software titles available.

The best option for tracking client time and building a profitable business is to consider the Industry Production Standards (ISP's). The ISP's are based on the average time required in the performance of specific duties for project production by a professional information processing operator, and calculated uniformly in 6-minute (0.1 hours) increments. They identify the time it would take an "average" person to complete the designated tasks, and provide you with PLUC charts to detail how to charge for these tasks based on the quality and quantity of work designated by the client. Although there are not detailed standards for some tasks and VA specialties, like desktop publishing, website development, and IT projects, these standards will help you develop pricing structures that will be fair and equitable for both you, and the client. You can get more information about the Standards at www.opac.com.

No matter which form of client time tracking works best for you, use it faithfully—it is vital in establishing and maintaining a profitable business.

Professional Image

Your professional image is conveyed in many ways—your marketing materials, your website, your business cards, your tagline, etc. Your "personal" professional image revolves around how you dress, how you groom and how you present yourself to those people you will meet at local meetings and events, as well as industry seminars and conventions.

When people see you dressed professionally, with a professional-looking haircut and accessories, it conveys a message to your potential clients that you take your business seriously. Always dress in business attire, unless you are aware of a "business casual" option for a specific event. Remember, you are a business owner, not someone's employee, and you should dress for your position!

Just as a client can hear your "smile" on the phone, they can sense how you feel about yourself. Especially as you are first starting out, force yourself to dress neatly and professionally, even if you'll just be sitting in front of your computer all day. Go through the same grooming ritual you would if you were going to work in an office somewhere. How you feel about yourself is most evident in how you present yourself. If dressing professionally every day is the best way to keep you motivated and feeling confident about yourself and your products/services, then dress for success every day!

Take this a step further when you have client or networking meetings. When you're in the company of others, they will notice what you're wearing. Is it professional? What about your body language? Is it confident and open? Are you speaking with a friendly tone and at an appropriate volume? Your professional image is not just about what you say, or how you dress, but how you present yourself.

In addition to how you dress and present yourself, your professional image comes across in other forms, like your marketing materials. Once you've established your company name and website, you'll want to post a professional logo. Unless you are a graphic artist, hire a professional to create something that will represent you in the best possible light. You can contact local professionals and try to find someone that could help you at a reasonable cost, or possibly even barter for services. If that fails, consider some of the more innovative options at very reasonable prices like, www.1800mylogo.com. They provide reasonably priced logos and provide you with a few options to choose from. You can save even more money if you have a detailed design or idea of what you want your logo to look like. You may also want to check within your VA associations to see if there is someone among the membership who has the skills you need to create a professional business logo. Being in the VA industry, they may have a better understanding of your needs.

Your brochure, letterhead, and business cards are also a big part of your professional image. Don't rely on your own inkjet printer to print out your letterhead and business cards. If price is a concern, look for reasonably priced options through local or online printers like, www.vistaprint.com or www.expresscopy.com. These companies will not only help you design or create a professional image, but can even work with your own designs. Printing services, as with many industries, vary in price and quality. If you can get a referral to a good service, this is probably your best option. Learning that the finished product is not up to your standards, after it's been printed, can be extremely costly.

Like it or not, we are judged by the image we present. You will be taken more seriously if you spend the money to have your business cards printed on heavy card stock by a professional printer. Your clients want to buy from the service provider who hands them the "Cadillac" of business cards and brochures. Make sure that's the image you present when you hand them these important marketing pieces about you and your business.

A final caution. Here's what "not" to discuss with your clients and colleagues. Even if your business is on the ropes, and you haven't done any client work in two months, never relay any negative information about your organization to anyone. If you're asked how business is, tell them it's, "doing well," even if it's not. If you leave the impression that you're not doing well, clients would be concerned about doing business with you because they might fear you may go out of business and they'll have to start over training a new service provider. Do not discuss any specific clients and their business practices or projects. Do not say anything negative about your competitors or clients. You never know who the person you're speaking to knows, or is acquainted with. Additionally, if you tell them something bad about another client, would they want to be your client and take the chance that you'll say something derogatory about them? Probably not!

Remember to act as a professional at all times. If you want to be an entrepreneur, you need to be one 24/7. It's okay to wear your grungiest clothes when working in the garden, but when you go out in public, even to the grocery store, make sure you are clean, presentable and neatly groomed—you never know where your next new client may come from. Always present yourself in the best way possible. It will go a long way in creating a professional image for you, and your growing practice.

The Executive Summary

Now you have created the identity for your business. You've named your business, designed your website and marketing materials, honed your 30 second commercial, identified your ideal client, and learned how to keep track of your time, been reminded how to project a professional image and discovered all the other little nuances that make your business uniquely yours.

The material presented in this chapter is certainly time-consuming and will require a lot of thought and creativity on your part, but once you finish with these items, you will be far ahead of so many other people starting out. Some VAs took years to have all the material in this chapter completed. But with all these tasks behind you, you're ready to learn how to find new clients and establish your business policies.

Chapter Links and Resources

Top Search Engines	www.google.com
	www.yahoo.com
	www.ask.com
	www.alltheweb.com
	www.search.aol.com
	www.hotbot.com
	www.altavista.com
	www.lycos.com
	www.bing.com
	www.vivisimo.com
	www.looksmart.com
Checking domain name availability	www.GoDaddy.com
	www.namecheap.com
	www.tigertech.net
To find out who owns a particular domain name	www.whosit.com
Website hosting options	www.GoDaddy.com
	www.TigerTech.net
	www.IPower.com
	www.gate.com
	www.hosting.com
	www.hostgator.com
	www.bluehost.com

Free association member hosting options	www.ivaa.org
Top Internet Browsers	www.InternetExplorer.com www.Aol.com www.Yahoo.com www.mozilla.com/firefox/ www.opera.com
Blog platform options:	www.wordpress.org www.blogger.com www.typepad.com
Social Media (top three)	www.Twitter.com www.Facebook.com www.LinkedIn.com
Pay scales and hourly wages	www.payscale.com www.bls.gov/bls/blswage.htm www.dol.gov/dol/topic/wages/
Online calendar/time management systems	www.intranets.com www.weboffice.com www.calendars.net www.trumba.com www.hyperoffice.com www.infostreet.com
Paper calendar/time management systems	www.franklincovey.com www.daytimer.com
Tracking client time	www.timeslips.com www.traxtime.com www.magsoftwrx.com/ www.sphericaltech.com www.responsivesoftware.com/

Project Management/ Time Tracking Options	www.basecamp.com
	www.Centraldesktop.com
	www.myclientspot.com
Industry Production Standards	www.obcai.com
Professional logo creation	www.1800mylogo.com
	www.logodesignpros.com
	www.logoworks.com
	www.businesslogos.com
	www.logodesignguru.com
Online printing options	www.vistaprint.com
	www.expresscopy.com
	www.imagegraphics.com
	www.bestprintingonline.com
	www.printingcenterusa.com
	www.modernpostcard.com

Sample Taglines

"An extra hand when you need one.™"
Linda Siniscal, Third Hand Secretarial Service™

"Out of sight business assistance."
Jackie Eastwick, Allison Lane Business Solutions

"Friendly Service, Professional Results Barbie Dallmann,"
Happy Fingers Word Processing and Business Services

"Making Dreams Come True" and *"If it sounds fun, we'll try it!"*
Marsha Wagner, CastleVisions

"Real solutions for real estate."
Caroline Wright, The Wright Solution

"Your Virtual Office Professionals"
Lisa Hoffman, Premier Administrative Services

"Let our office be your office."
Marlene McCall, Creative Office Services

"Partridge Typing & Print, Ltd., the name that clients and companies recommend."
Faye Partridge, Partridge Typing & Print, Ltd.

"Innovative Solutions for Your Business Support Needs"
Janice Wlodarski, Progressive Publishing Services

"At your side; not under your feet."
JudyAnn Lorenz, Bar JD Communications

"We take care of the work, so you can take care of business."
Heather Lee, design/type

"Professional and Confidential Secretarial & Mailing Services – Done Fast! Done Right!"
Vicki L. Duncan, Duncan Business Services, Inc.

"Give US the runaround" and *'Turning chaos into order"*
Katie Baird, Loose Ends

"I don't really have a tagline; my business name says it all."
Sandy Giusti, Consider it Done Virtual Assistant Services

Chapter Four

How To Find And Keep Clients

One of the biggest questions new VAs ask is, "How can I find new clients?" Unfortunately, there's no easy answer. You will find your clients from a combination of efforts—advertising, networking, referrals, marketing, rekindling past connections and word-of-mouth. Building a full-time client load takes some time, so you need to keep up your momentum.

Once you find your clients, you need to know how to work with them so your relationship continues to be a win-win situation for both of you. You'll need to know when to refuse work or cut your losses, and how to handle sticky situations like client objections.

This chapter covers some of the main client issues you may face, both in finding clients and in keeping them. Knowledge is power, as they say, so by knowing ahead of time what may crop up, you will be better prepared to solve any problems.

Networking Groups Online and Off

Networking is one of the most important marketing tools for your small business. Whether networking online or off, getting the message out about what you do—and who you serve—is vital to your success.

Networking in-person is a great way to get your feet wet. Contact your local Chamber office, or another one in a larger metropolitan area near you, to find out when they meet. Most Chambers meet once a month at a local restaurant. This is a great place to network and get a feel for the types of businesses in your immediate area.

Ask around about a local Rotary, Kiwanis, or Optimist Club. These organizations are International Civic groups that have local Chapters consisting mainly of local business people. For those of you who struggle to 'speak' at such functions, consider joining Toastmasters. They have local chapters nationwide that will help you overcome your shyness and help you master speaking in front of a crowd while also being an option for prospective clients.

Check online for local chapters of organizations that have a general membership, like NAWBO (National Association of Women Business Owners), eWomenNetwork.com, or groups that may be hangouts for prospects in your niche, like the Women's Council of Realtors (WCR). All of these organizations have memberships open to men and women.

Research local leads groups, like BNI (Business Network International), and other organizations that may have good connections to prospective clients. Your area may also have independent leads groups. Do a website search or check in the local business journals and newspapers for calendar items and announcements of business group events.

Membership and event fees for all these organizations can get pricey. Most groups will allow you to attend their meetings once or twice for free or for a nominal cost. Attend one where you will benefit from the meeting topic and use these meetings wisely. Or if the topic speaks to the type of prospect or projects you'd enjoy working on, this would also mean that the audience has an interest, or has challenges in these areas that you may be able to solve.

> "I find my local clients get to know me a little better simply by virtue of actually being in the same room once in a while. I enjoy picking up or dropping off work on occasion - I've noticed nearly all of my clients have excellent senses of humor, so being around them is actually a joy many times."
> Jackie Eastwick, Allison Lane Business Solutions

It will be a great opportunity to hone your networking skills. You may even find an immediate connection to a client, someone willing to mentor you, or someone who will refer you to someone they know who could use your product or service. Once you have tried a few, depending on your budget, join the ones that connect you to the broadest segment of prospects, or people in industries that you feel could be a good resource for referral business.

Especially when networking "live," you will probably be required to be the "educator." Virtual businesses are still somewhat new, so, depending on where you live, you may need to explain your business, plus how you work. Be sure to tell even local clients that you work virtually, too. With today's more mobile society, many of your local clients will know other people across the country whom they could refer you to. You must find creative ways to reach your audience, and make the connection memorable.

Online networking is a much different animal. For those who find a face-to-face encounter somewhat challenging, online networking can provide a safety net and give you the chance to build your courage, and self-esteem, to make "live" networking easier to tackle.

Start by finding industry associations that are "virtual" in nature. Some you may consider are the International Virtual Assistants Association (IVAA), the Virtual Assistant Network (vanetworking.com), or the Alliance for Virtual Businesses. These are all great places to find other VAs who are willing to share their experiences, lend a hand, and provide support to anyone with a problem or question. They usually have some sort of list-serv that will allow you the ability to "lurk" and see what everyone else is doing, or get involved and participate with a question or respond to someone else's request. You will find more information about these groups and their URL's at the end of this Chapter.

Other great online communities would include 'business' groups, like businessknowhow.com, which have message boards and chat rooms where business owners meet to discuss all kinds of things. Run a "business" search at yahoogroups.com for groups of small businesspeople who may have list-serves where businesspeople gather to discuss the ins and outs of running a profitable business.

If you specialize in a particular market segment, like real estate, bookkeeping, coaches, speakers, authors, web designers, etc., check the major search engines for opportunities to find where those particular potential clients, or colleagues may congregate online.

Social Media Networks

Social Media has been on the scene now for only several years, but has created an option with Internet networking that reaches a broader target. Use these options to connect specifically to your niche or target market, other virtual assistants, and groups that allow you to capture and connect with others that will bring in new prospects while also helping you to understand the challenges your niche market faces, which could help you expand your business into new income streams.

Let's say you join a coaches group on LinkedIn–your goal will be to answer their questions and solve some of their challenges to help establish your expertise. What you may also find compelling is that you will see some common threads in their challenges – in this case, perhaps many of them are asking questions about shopping carts, how to manage the autoresponders, how to setup the cart with their logo, etc. This allows you an option to expand your services to offer support in these areas that seem to be a challenge to many coaches. You may not have ever considered offering shopping cart support had you not experienced first-hand that they struggle with managing this software in their business.

Unlike when social media first became popular, we do not suggest that you 'connect' to everyone. Be sure that you connect with only those people who have a connection to you personally or professionally. Be open to involvement in multiple group environments that will help you to establish or expand your expertise by being a resource and answering questions.

These platforms can not only be great referral and prospect resources, but help you to better understand your clients' challenges and needs.

How Exactly Do You Network?

Now that you've found all these great places to network, what's next? What can you do to make your networking the most effective time you spend? Better yet, let's cover what you should NOT do. Networking is not about passing your business card out to as many people as possible. It's not about spouting your 60-second infomercial and moving on to the next victim. Networking is about listening, sharing, and caring to solve someone else's need.

> *"Networking, networking, and more networking via business and personal channels, along with some volunteering. Two-way word-of-mouth referrals are also great and beneficial!"*
>
> Lisa Hoffman, Premier Administrative Services

The best networking events (whether live or online) are the ones in which you are able to listen to someone's need, and help them resolve the problem. Even if it's something that has nothing at all to do with your business, try to provide a solution. If someone is looking for a good kennel to keep her dogs while she is on vacation, and you know one, hand her your card with the name of a local kennel you suggest written on the back. If you don't have the contact information with you, ask for one of her cards, and let her know you'll forward the information to her.

Networking is about building relationships, and finding commonalities that will help you build a network of associates who will become your best advocates as the relationships grow. If you are the giver and they are the receiver, the relationship will grow more quickly; especially if you need to polish your infomercial. What better way to break the ice than to introduce yourself, and ask the other person what they do? Online, get involved with chats that may offer you the opportunity to provide help or support to someone who has a need you can fill…even if it's not a business need. Help with as many needs as you can and you will come to the top of their mind the next time someone has a need that fits your skill set, or really, any need at all.

The advantage to this is that as your business grows, it will most likely change. You may add products or services that you have not communicated to all of your networking associates, so knowing that they will connect with you whenever a need arises, leaves you open to offer connections to new associations, or expand your business by offering additional services that may now fill their needs.

Once you've shown that you are a good listener and concerned about them and their needs, the natural response is for them to reciprocate. If they do not, they're not a good networker, and probably not interested in building a relationship. Cut your losses and move on to someone else.

Networking comes in all sizes and shapes. The more you do, the easier it gets. The more people in your network, the better job they do as your "sales force" to spread the word about what you can do to make others' lives easier. The more you give of yourself, the more you will gain in return. If you have provided good qualified leads to people in your network, they will go out of their way to find business leads for you. Those are the types of relationships you are looking to build. Building good networking relationships takes time. This is especially true online because you don't have that face-to-face component, but be patient and take the time to be a good, and consistent, networker.

Building your business by referral through networking will provide you with a more qualified clientele. They will already be sold on your product or service and ready to sign on the dotted line.

Taking Networking One Step Further

Two other options for expanding your network would be to consider being a speaker, and/or writing business related articles. There's no better way to set yourself up as the 'expert' than to be called upon to speak on a related business topic, and/or writing articles that will make you more identifiable in the business community.

You may not find the VA Industry as a viable topic for discussion, but find a niche that you can speak or write professionally about, that will allow those who hear or read your words to leave with some knowledge and information that may benefit them, and leave them hungry for more.

Many of the organizations mentioned in the previous section, local Chambers, Kiwanis, Rotary, and Optimist Clubs, are always looking for speakers for their meetings. Local business magazines, newspapers and business group newsletters also could use business-related articles which provide you with a byline, and in some cases, a short bio or link to your website.

Topics to consider may include: marketing ideas and tips, the importance of a website, the advantages of outsourcing, tips and tricks for basic software programs (this can be especially beneficial when targeting a specific niche, like real estate – you can give them tips and tricks for industry specific software that they use every day), which will communicate your knowledge and expertise, which may translate into a business relationship to benefit you both.

Writing a few articles, or speaking to small business groups is an inexpensive way to tout your business knowledge and ethics, while educating potential clients on the advantages of working with you. Even if you're not able to completely incorporate your virtual business into the presentation or article, you will generate interest in finding out more about you and the products or services you provide.

Overcoming Client Objections

Client objections come in all sizes and shapes. From the client interview all the way through to project completion and paying your invoice, how you react to a client objection is a great way to learn the ins and outs of running a business.

Sounds strange, doesn't it? Strange, but absolutely true. As with most things, we learn by doing, and sometimes we don't have the answer until we've experienced the question. Trying to consider client objections before they're asked is always helpful, but clients are always coming up with new objections and we can't cover them all in this book!

Some, however, are more common than others.

Price:

You pick-up the phone, or get an e-mail asking for your rates. You quote the price, and the potential client gives you the impression that your pricing is outrageous. So what should you do? Instead of quoting them a price, take control of the conversation by asking them a series of questions that will help you better understand what they're looking for, and help them better understand that you are a professional and know what you're talking about.

> *"I frankly don't encounter too many client objections, probably because I spend a lot of time during the initial contact establishing my expertise. Once we've completed that conversation, the majority of prospects book the project. If I sense that price is their main concern, I clarify that immediately and offer to refer them to someone whose rates are lower than mine."*
>
> Heather Lee, design/type

Get as much detail as you possibly can, and if possible, ask for a sample of the way the completed project should look, or a sample of how the data needed to complete the project will be provided. This will not only give you a better idea of how to quote the project, but will also give you an indication of the professionalism of the potential client.

As you take your time to get more information to give the potential client an informed decision, you are successfully building a rapport with them, and giving them the idea that they're speaking to a professional businessperson. Then, when quoting them the price, detail for them what is involved, and how you will handle their project. This may help you in alleviating a client's first potential objection—price. If not, you have been successful in weeding out someone who may not be a good potential client for you.

Working Virtually

Another common objection by clients is that you're working "virtually." People tend to feel that if they're not watching you do the work, how can they trust that it actually took you three hours to complete it and not two? How do they know you weren't watching the soaps and eating bon-bons?

Responding to the "virtual" objection depends on a few things: One, are they local to you? Do they live or work within driving distance where they could actually expect you to do the work from their office or are they far enough away that this would be impossible, and that is why they're hesitant to hire you? Without knowing the reason for the objection, you can't respond correctly to reassure them.

For anyone with this objection, a client reference is usually a good place to start. If you don't have a current client to refer them to, how about a former employer, or co-worker who could give you a glowing reference and help them feel more comfortable? You may also consider offering them their first hour or two free, just so they can get a feel for what you can produce for them, virtually. And of course, if they do live within driving distance, you may also consider doing the work from their office, but be sure to add something to your hourly rate.

If you're first starting out, it may be difficult to turn away this "on-site" business, especially if it meets your skill-set. But be sure that you compensate for the fact that you will have additional expenses involved in getting to and from their office; you may be working within another "city" or "township" that would require you to pay local taxes for any work done within their city limits; you are also away from your office so you are unable to work on other client projects in the background, like making copies, or printing postcards, or any of a number of things that could be accomplished while you are doing this client's project; or, you may miss a call from a prospective client.

Having a higher rate to do on-site work can also be a deterrent to clients who want to have more control over your business. If you desire to work 'virtually,' you must be sure to maintain control of your business, and not allow a client to dictate or change your business focus. And if you are willing to work outside of your normal practices, they should pay you a higher fee to do so.

On-site work also presents the possibility that the client will treat you as an employee. Remember, this is your business, you make the rules. You are an independent contractor and in order for the client to avoid any exposure to employment taxes and insurance, they need to understand the relationship. Be clear with any client you work for on-site and maintain a professional business-to-business relationship at all times.

Timing

Be clear about project turn-around time and do not be swayed by a client who simply MUST have it completed in a less than reasonable amount of time. Be firm, and offer options to complete the project on time, consider hiring sub-contractors to assist you in completing the project, or offer to work overtime at an increased rate to complete it within their guidelines. Be wary of continually offering clients the opportunity to make unreasonable demands. You will again be giving them the ability to consider you an employee, rather than an independent contractor. It will cause a lot of disruption in the growth and success of your business, and could hurt the future of your company. Allowing clients too much control over your business will translate into additional difficulties down the road. This is your business—you decide how it will operate—no one else.

You will undoubtedly find new and unique client objections the longer you are in business. You will learn to effectively handle each client objection as it presents itself. With experience, you will learn that client objections can be a wonderful insight into how to work better and more efficiently for all your clients. Take the time to listen carefully to what the client is communicating and take your time in responding. Ask questions if you need something clarified. Don't shoot from the hip; be willing to consider their side of the objection and reply rationally.

Good clients will always be willing to consider their options and look at both sides of a situation. If you're uncertain how to respond, ask more questions about the objection so you can consider the most positive response.

Keeping the communication open is of the utmost importance. Sometimes client objections will throw you off guard. Remain calm and think before you respond. Even if you don't give the perfect answer this time, you'll be better prepared and ready for action the next time that objection is voiced.

Client objections are a great way to learn, and if you consider handling them as an opportunity, you may find that you welcome some objections in order to better understand your business profile, and what it is about your business that you enjoy doing, and those things that you will eventually outsource to someone else.

Communicating With Clients

Client projects can be communicated in many ways. The most common are by e-mail, fax, snail mail, voice recording, diskette or CD, or online file sharing.

As technology continues to advance, client projects may now be uploaded to Internet-based systems where we can then retrieve them. Or you can utilize software such as GoToMyPC, or PCAnywhere, which allow you to login to a client's computer and work on their projects "live," or even network to a client's server so that you have access to their files and even print them on their printer.

Whatever method you and your client choose to communicate, be certain you have clear instructions of what the client expects. Communicating during the project is just as important as the way the client initially delivers the project to you. Don't be afraid to ask questions, or to forward a sample of the work in progress, to make certain you are proceeding as the client expects.

"The best marketing for me is good customer service. I meet client deadlines and meet or exceed their expectations on the work performed for them. I send gifts to my clients at least once a year, and they're always well received. Now my clients are 100% referral. And the referrals I get are great clients. It takes much less work and much less money to keep a client than to get a new client."

Kathy Mandy, Select Word Services

Take the time to understand how each client prefers to communicate. Understanding the client's preferred communication style will assist you in building a long-lasting relationship and good client base. Some clients will prefer communicating details by phone, as they understand better audibly, some clients prefer to "see" what you're saying, and find visual communications, like emails, documents and file sharing easier to understand.

As an entrepreneur, you must learn to communicate with many different types of people in all walks of life. As a virtual assistant, it is quite probable that you will be dealing with clients all over the country and quite possibly all over the world. Sharpening your senses to understand each client's individual communication style will help you differentiate yourself from the competition.

Handling Difficult Clients

Being "virtual" often attracts potential clients who are not accustomed to working with someone who is more of a partner than an employee. This may create conflicts that are literally beyond anyone's ability to solve reasonably.

Some clients want something for nothing—they believe that because you work at home you have no overhead, and should be at their beck and call 24/7. Some VAs offer this level of support, many do not. Some clients expect that you will require no training or information at all, because you market yourself as an "expert" in particular niche markets, or with particular software programs.

However, it's unlikely that you would know the inner workings of their business, and although you may have experience with a particular software program, most software has features and benefits that many of us are unaware of and this difficult client may use them. Don't let such a client 'bully' you. They are simply not worth the extra time and effort it will take to try and satisfy them. There will be clients you just cannot satisfy—no matter what you do.

> "One client attempted to take advantage of my staff by giving unreasonable instructions and berating them in a demanding, derogatory manner instead of contacting me. After listening to her complaint and the description of the incident by staff, I promptly informed the client that she needed to find someone else to handle her work."
>
> Sharon Williams,
> The 24-Hour Secretary

If you have the misfortune of working for a client like this, you are better off completing the task to the best of your ability, and accepting no payment in return. Yes, work for free. Think about it: If the client is unhappy with your work, you run the risk of them tarnishing your reputation to their friends and colleagues, and possibly irreparably damaging your business. No amount of money the client could pay you could repair such damage. You are always better off taking the "high road", and putting yourself in their shoes. Consider how you would react if the tables were turned. Would you expect to pay for the project? Could you create a win-win, by asking just for your actual expenses, like printing or postage, etc., and part amicably? Don't look at it as admitting defeat; consider it cutting your losses.

When you work "in person" you have more criteria on which to judge the prospective client. You often get a "gut feeling" when dealing with people that is tougher to get when working virtually. Therefore, it is sometimes difficult to weed out unethical people. And if they're unethical enough to take advantage of you, why wouldn't they be unethical enough to try and tarnish your reputation?

By offering clients a 100% guarantee on your work, you remove their ability to do much damage. How could they complain when you worked for them for free? Some will try, but you can simply respond by saying they were unhappy with the work so you didn't charge them…then who looks like the bad guy? If you accept payment, you're indicating that the job was done to their satisfaction. If it wasn't, it makes it easier for them to get support from their friends and colleagues that you were at fault. Taking the high road usually deflates their ego, and makes them back down. A 100% satisfaction guarantee is a great investment in keeping your reputation intact, and a tax write-off, too.

Local Businesses Versus Virtual Clients

Believe it or not, enough businesses exist—locally, and virtually—to keep everyone busy for a long time. The hard part is finding the right work to fit your skills and those that will be the most challenging. There are no hard and fast rules about whether virtual or local business is better, or where the best business for you will be found.

Depending on the area of the world in which you live, you may find that local business is far less profitable than virtual business. Your business expenses for Internet access, telephone service, office supplies, office or housing costs, etc., can be dramatically different depending on your location.

Use the Internet as a tool to research the cost of living in your area, and compare them to other areas of the world where clients can be found. This knowledge will help you decide where to spend the bulk of your marketing dollars, and even help you decide on a specialty.

You may also find that local business requires a little more of your time, as clients may stop by your office, or prefer to deliver projects over lunch. However, locally, you may have less competition than in the virtual world. Doing your homework will give you the knowledge to help you decide what your client base might look like, and how to keep the best balance of local and virtual clients.

Don't put all your eggs into one basket. Always continue to market and promote your business on both levels. As your business evolves and as you find your niche, having some good basic research on these two areas of business opportunities will help you realize the most profitable options for your products and services for many years to come.

Ethics and Customer Service

In some ways, you must have higher customer service standards in a virtual world than will be required with local clients. There is still some basic distrust of virtual businesses because the industry is so young, and there has not been a lot of available information on good business practices.

There will always be "bad" business people in every industry, but when an industry is first taking shape, there is a tendency to attract unscrupulous individuals who have no intention of running a stable, ethical business. "Say, I can balance my checkbook in QuickBooks, why couldn't I charge someone to do their bookkeeping?" They will eventually, (and usually quickly), go out of business, but this is still very damaging to the client base that are usually timid in taking the "virtual" plunge.

For this reason, set very high service standards to differentiate yourself and help solidify the industry. As you and others like you set the standards of excellence, the rest will follow. This will help make the industry stronger and allow us to operate thriving businesses.

Having strong customer service skills will help grow your business and your reputation. Customer service is the most important benefit that a potential client is looking for, higher on the list than project delivery and price.

Create and implement a customer service pledge to your clients, and make it your mission to be sure that each and every client knows that it's your goal to make them satisfied with everything you do for them. You have a vested interest in making them successful by providing them with top-notch products or services. If you cannot provide them with the highest level of service, they will have no reason to continue to do business with you, or equally important, refer business to you.

Much of what you have already read about planning and implementing your business in this book can help you to understand the level of service required to stay at the top of your game. In a nutshell, make the client feel like they have your undivided attention, that although you both know they're not your only client; you should make them feel as if they are. They should understand that you are their biggest supporter, and you will do whatever it takes to make sure that you provide them with the utmost in professional products or services to fit their needs.

Periodically, perhaps once or twice a year, browse your customer service plan and update it or expand it where necessary. Consider taking inexpensive online or local classes in customer service to increase your knowledge and add value to your plan. Include this process when finalizing content for your brochure or your website homepage. Clients will appreciate and understand how valuable customer service is to their bottom line; they will find you more trustworthy and professional if you communicate how important customer service is to you. Just one more advantage to building a relationship with you.

Saying "No" To a Potential Client

Do not to take on any client projects that do not meet your skill set. Do not overstate your experience or abilities as this could be disastrous to your ego and your business. You will also encounter clients who just don't understand the concept of working with an independent contractor, or are looking to take advantage of you.

Establish your business practices and criteria early on, and stick to the plan. Taking projects outside your comfort and skill zone will cause much larger long-term problems with your reputation and style of doing business. Set boundaries for yourself and stay comfortably within them.

> *"In instances where I need to say, 'no' to a client, I have simply stated that my schedule did not allow for me to take on any other projects. In an instance where I needed to fire a client, I basically informed them of my rate increase knowing that they would not be willing to pay the current rate, and being an occasional client, our relationship quietly ended."*
>
> Janice Wlodarski,
> Progressive Publishing Services

If you consistently take on the wrong types of clients, those same types of clients will be referred to you, and you will find you are extremely busy doing work you don't like and not making a profit.

Learn to say "no", and mean it! There are ways to say no to a potential client without being rude or insensitive. Consider some of these options to help soften the blow:

- I have no experience with this type of project work.
- I don't believe we are a good fit for each other.
- That project isn't a good fit for me. You may want to post this opportunity on eLance or guru.com where freelance workers can bid on the job.

- I've changed the focus of my business and am only accepting clients in (name a specific industry of which they do not belong).
- I have taken on a rather large project and am not able to take on any new projects at this time.

Learning to say no to business that doesn't fit your practice is a big step in creating an ethical and successful business. You will establish yourself as a qualified and knowledgeable business owner with your clients, peers, and colleagues.

Firing Clients

As in any business environment, there will be instances when you will need to "fire" a client. You may change your business focus; your client may change his or her needs; be consistently slow to pay, continually make deductions from invoices; create a conflict of interest with another of your client's businesses; or experience a shift in management to someone who isn't a good fit for your business style and focus.

Whatever the case might be, find the most compassionate option to sever the relationship. If appropriate, find someone else to refer them to who can pick up where you leave off. Commit to completing any pending projects, and give them adequate notice. Two weeks is usually sufficient.

> "One of our favorite ways to 'fire' a client is to say, 'If price is your only consideration, perhaps we're not the service for you.' We believe we bring a lot of quality, integrity and expertise to every project and our clients are spoiled with our customer service."
>
> Vicki L. Duncan,
> Duncan Business Services, Inc.

Remember, you want to have even the fired client walk away feeling they were enriched by the experience, and have a high regard for you and the VA industry. Even if it's a bad situation and you're within your rights to really let them have it—don't. This doesn't accomplish anything and creates bad feelings. No one likes or anticipates being fired. Remember to put yourself in their place, and imagine how you'd feel and react if you were the one being fired.

Firing clients is just a part of being in business. It's nothing you plan for, but sometimes a necessity to move your business forward. Treat it as a normal part of doing business, and handle it as a professional. You'll feel much better after you do it and you will establish a high level of respect for yourself and your business.

Collections

You've gotten your business set up, applied your brand, found some great clients, and now you're waiting patiently to be paid....30-days has passed, now what?

Thirty days is probably the maximum amount of time you should extend to a client to pay for project work. In the early stages of your practice, especially with virtual clients, you may want to consider requiring half up front, and half upon completion until you are able to establish a working client relationship. In most cases, you should consider making your business model for invoice payments as "due upon receipt." Although you would give those clients up to 30-days to pay, setting these terms, allows you additional flexibility in the collections process. You may also want to consider detailing your terms in your Work for Hire Agreement. That way, you have the client's signature to verify they understood the terms of payment.

If you're going to consider securing government work, know up front that they are slow to pay. To avoid this problem, you may want to offer 1%-10, net 30-day terms, as the government is required to pay within terms only if a discount is provided. In some cases, as little as $1/2$ of 1% is considered enough of a discount to allow prompt payment.

Another option would be to consider working with clients on "retainer." Clients on retainer purchase a set number of hours, per week, or per month, and pay you in advance for those hours. This allows them the luxury of having their projects done prior to any "as needed," or invoiced after the project is completed, because they have paid you in advance to get top priority. Some VAs offer retainer hours at a discount, but many do not. The advantage to the client is the ability to get top priority.

> "I tell the client, 'I would certainly go with them if I were you, since you're looking for a bargain and their rate is so much below what most people are charging. However, if you end up unhappy with the quality or reliability of that person, or you have any communication problems with them, do feel free to call us back.'"
>
> Nina Feldman, Nina Feldman Connections

For those projects that are not paid up front, you may find yourself in a position to have to ask for payment. As you setup your business practices, prepare guidelines for client payment and receivables. Treat all clients the same, and detail exactly how you will handle delinquent accounts.

Perhaps you initiate a phone call, follow that with a letter, and finally an e-mail. Trying to collect on receivables on your own will save you 10-20% in the total invoice amount, if you would be forced to turn them over to collections. Once an invoice has gotten to 45-days, it would be wise to hold off doing any additional client work unless the client has given you a clear indication of when the invoice will be paid.

Once an invoice is beyond 90-days and you have no concrete commitment for payment from the client, it may be wise to consider turning them over to collections so that you will not spend more of your valuable time on someone who may be wasting it.

Shop around for a good collections person, as you would for any product or service. The best option would be to get a referral from someone who successfully uses such a service in their business. Some virtual assistants even provide collections services. Don't forget to support your fellow VAs if one offers a service you can use.

The Executive Summary

This chapter has taken us from identifying where you might be able to connect with potential clients, to how to collect your money when they won't pay. Dealing with clients is one area where you get better with experience. Keep in mind the 80/20 rule: 80% of your income will come from 20% of your clients. You want to identify that 20% early on so that you can make sure you're not in a situation where you're spending 80% of your time on a client who represents 20% of your income.

In time, you'll learn which clients are the best fits for you and which ones you need to avoid. Realize that, with clients, you don't need to look for people who could be your best friends, but they should respect your expertise, your time, and the way you run your business. Even veteran VAs will run into client problems occasionally, so when they occur, refer to this chapter for ideas on how to handle them.

Chapter Links and Resources

Networking Organizations

www.uschamber.com

www.rotary.org

www.kiwanis.org

www.optimist.org

www.bni.com

www.nawbo.org

www.wcr.org

www.eWomenNetwork.com

www.aipb.com (Bookkeepers)

Virtual Assistant/Business Organizations

www.ivaa.org

www.vanetworking.com

www.iava.org.uk (United Kingdom)

www.Staffcentrix.com (Military Spouses)

www.cvac.ca (Canada)

www.allianceforvirtualbiz.com

www.va4u.com (Australia)

www.asecretary.com.au (Australia)

Business Information & Networking

www.businessknowhow.com

www.bspage.com (Your Business Start Page)

www.myownbusiness.com

www.totalbusiness.com

www.startinbusiness.co.uk/ (UK)

www.startingabusinessinireland.com/ (Ireland)

www.ryze.com

www.ecademy.com

Social Media Networking   www.twitter.com

www.twibes.com

www.LinkedIn.com

www.Facebook.com

www.Plaxo.com

Communicating with   www.gotomypc.com
a Client's computer
www.pcanywhere.com

www.pcnow.com

www.logmein.com

www.networkstreaming.com

http://pcnow.webex.com

Chapter Five

Professional Development

*I*f you worked for a Fortune 500 company, you'd regularly be sent to professional development trainings—conferences, seminars, classes, etc. Now, you are the person who gets to decide which training you should get and how often.

This is not an area to skimp on with your budget. Independent professionals need this type of professional development at least as often as those who work for other companies. Professional development helps you learn new technologies, new processes, and new ways of doing business.

Professional development can be as simple as picking up a book or as involved as traveling across the country to attend a conference. It can be listening to a lecture or studying for a certification test.

In this chapter we will explore some professional development options ranging from inexpensive to pricey and ideas of where to find them.

Continuing Education

Although you have the skills and knowledge needed to perform the services you plan to provide, working virtually is still a relatively new concept. It's one that requires continual growth and development—no matter how many years of experience you may have.

Initially, you may need to consider updating your skills to meet the needs of the marketplace. This may include researching the most up-to-date software programs your proposed market segment is using, as well as, learning the more advanced features and benefits of some of the software programs you mistakenly believed you were completely familiar with.

Providing references helps potential clients feel more confident in your abilities. As a new business, though, you won't necessarily be able to provide them. Taking continuing education classes will help bridge that gap, and provide you and your clients with confirmation and validation of your skill level. This will go far in communicating to clients not only your abilities, but your desire to stay current with industry trends and software updates, and minimize their need to address these ongoing issues with you.

Remember, you are looking to provide them with the most up-to-date products and services from an entrepreneurial standpoint, not that of an employee. It will be your on-going responsibility to take a leadership role in the future needs of your market segment. By being that "experienced" resource, you communicate to your clients that you are the expert, and that they can come to you for all the information they need to keep their business running smoothly and profitably. You will ultimately benefit, because your clients will always come to you first whenever they have a question or need information about what products and services are available to them that will help them increase their productivity.

> "Each year I have learned a new software program, gotten a professional license or a VA designation. In addition, I also attend the IVAA Summit each year, which serves several purposes: the presentations themselves provide educational opportunities; networking with other VAs provides growth and on a personal level, the opportunity to annually review my company's progress since the last Summit and set goals for the new year."
>
> Caroline Wright, The Wright Solution

Continuing education is not only for "new" business owners, but seasoned VAs as well. As your business starts to grow and evolve, many times you will find that you will be changing your focus, and/or profit centers to better meet the needs of your clientele. Many times this translates into gaining knowledge about new technology and services that will increase productivity for you, and your clients. This is a never-ending process for a savvy, seasoned VA. As you become more successful, you will be able to outsource some of that continuing research to other VAs or "experts" in current trends and technologies.

There are many options for continuing education, whether from a local community college, your community recreation association, specialized training facilities such as New Horizons, or through online portals to colleges and universities worldwide. As the virtual assistance industry has continued to evolve, there are even new specialized training options available for specific types of services that VAs can offer.

Taking the time to increase your knowledge base and taking the necessary steps to acquire additional training will also help clients find more value in your products and services, which will make taking regular price increases a normal function of the growth of your business.

Some specialized online VA training programs we highly recommend are: AssistU (www.Assistu.com), VAClassroom (www.VAclassroom.com), Virtual Business Training (www.virtualbusinesstraining.com), and Virtual Assistant University, VAU (www.virtualassistanceu.com). For basic business training, try Small Business U (www.Smallbizu.com).

PROFESSIONAL DEVELOPMENT   83

Industry and Small Business Conferences

To continue your business success, it's always important to stay abreast of new technologies and practices that can positively or negatively impact the way you do business and how you compete within the marketplace.

The rewards of attending conferences are far-reaching. You can hone your skills and learn about new products and technologies. These will help you increase your knowledge, your client's productivity and increase your bottom line. One of the biggest benefits of attending conferences is to mingle with other successful business owners and peers who can help guide and support you throughout your career. The long-term relationships you build will be priceless. It also helps to get you outside of your cozy and sometimes isolating home office.

Although at the present time we find only two viable options geared specifically towards the VA industry, the IVAA Best Practices Summit (one live and one online) (www.vasummit.org), and the Alliance for Virtual Businesses' webinar (www.OIVAC.com), there are many other opportunities locally, nationally, and globally, that can offer you the opportunity to expand your knowledge of our industry. They'll also provide you with information on the latest trends in running a business, marketing, networking, and continuing to grow on a personal and professional level.

A quick Google search for "business conferences" will yield a plethora of opportunities for professional growth. Checking the 'events' through your local Chamber, Small Business Administration Office, or through national and global organizations like NAWBO (National Association of Women Business Owners), and WorldWIT (Women, Insights, Technology) will connect you to conference opportunities that will fit your every need.

> *"When people ask me what has allowed me to stay in business over 20-years, while so many other office service owners and VAs have gone back to being employed by someone else, I attribute it to the support I've gotten from the professional VA associations I participate in, and the sense of belonging to a professional industry larger than just my own little home business, as well as networking with my local peers."*
>
> Nina Feldman,
> Nina Feldman Connections

"Never stop learning" are certainly words to live by when owning and operating a VA practice. Take every opportunity you can to expand your knowledge base and continue to evolve and grow your business into the perfect fit for you and your client base. Use this time to rejuvenate you and your business, and build relationships with peers and mentors that will provide you with a lifetime of support and encouragement second to none.

Attending conferences is a "must" to maintain and grow a profitable business. Get involved, and make the investment in yourself and your business that conferences will provide.

Certifications

Certifications are an important tool in your VA practice. This is what separates you from your competition, and broadcasts your expertise to potential and current clients. For those of you who will be specializing in your VA practice, certifications are a must.

Do some extensive research to make sure you are spending your dollars wisely, not only from a testing standpoint, but from an "acceptance" standpoint.

Is the particular certification you hope to achieve well accepted by the clientele you hope to serve? Does the certification program allow you on-going support and PR to your target market? Does your certification allow you a directory type listing at appropriate websites that will be available to your target market? Is there a logo for this certification program that you can post at your website? Can you speak to those who have already achieved the certification to assess the value of the program in their business?

> "Depending upon what niche (if any) a new VA is exploring, there are many educational and certification possibilities out there to assist in putting your 'best self and package' forward. The key is to stay current, and investigate/pursue making them part of your repertoire."
>
> Lisa Hoffman, Premier Administrative Services

Once you've decided on the best certifications to fit your business, make sure that you find out about any study guides that may be available to you, prior to taking the test(s). If there aren't any study guides, ask for any additional information about the test format and any materials they might suggest you use prior to taking the test.

After you have achieved the designations, be certain to use them in your marketing materials, at your website, and even in your e-mail signatures. Don't miss an opportunity to open a dialog with a potential client who is curious by all those acronyms behind your name.

Certifications are another good way to communicate your advanced skills and knowledge of your industry that helps clients understand they are truly working with an expert. You will find that when faced with a decision to choose a VA, Certifications will go far in helping to differentiate yourself from the competition. It also continues to add credence to your pricing

Professional Development

structure. People will expect and be willing to pay more for your products and services in some part because of your dedication to continuing education and certifications.

Professional Associations

Belonging to professional associations is a sure sign that you are confident and polished. Many of these organizations also provide you with great networking opportunities to further develop professionally and personally.

Whatever your specialty or skill set, there is sure to be an association that caters to others who share your passions and expertise. Being a part of such associations helps strengthen your industry, and will assist you in bringing more credibility to your business and the industry as a whole. In doing so, clients will feel more comfortable with the VA industry overall, and make your job easier, by educating and "selling" them on your products and/or services.

For example, someone with a CPA designation doesn't need to explain or educate their potential clients in their abilities or what skills they bring to the table. In time, VA certifications will be understood in the same way. As the Virtual Assistant industry becomes more recognized, so will your certifications.

Some professional VA organizations include, the International Virtual Assistants Association (www.IVAA.org), the Virtual Assistant Network (www.vanetworking.com), and the Alliance for Virtual Businesses (www.allianceforvirtualbiz.com).

If you have a VA specialization, take the certification process one step further. For example, if you specialize in Realtor support, find out if you have a local Chapter of WCR (Women's Council of Realtors), or contact your local real estate Board to see if they have business expos, or educational seminars that you could provide some "free" educational information as it relates to their industry and/or your particular product or service. Business expos usually provide you with the ability to secure booth space, which is a great way to strut your stuff, and get out in front of an audience that you are looking to connect with.

> *"Belonging to professional associations is essential. I think there are other good organizations besides IVAA. I do not have the energy to give to more than one and I am quite satisfied with IVAA. Volunteering – give to get."*
>
> JudyAnn Lorenz,
> Bar JD Communications

If bookkeeping is your game, find out if you have a local CPA organization that might be a good fit for you. Although you may not be a CPA, you may be able to offer basic services their clients need, but their clients may find difficult to afford at the CPA's rates. This gives you an opportunity to allow that CPA to offer these services to benefit their clients, and create a win-win-win by doing so.

If your specialty is servicing coaches and professional speakers, join the local NSA (National Speaker's Association), and volunteer some of your time utilizing your skills that would translate into VA support to them.

Being a member of one or more of these industry associations is a wise investment in your business. It communicates to clients that you're serious about your business, and your industry, which means you will be there to serve them for many years to come. In almost every industry, there are those that are in it for a quick buck, and usually move on or out of business just as quickly. Being involved in the industry gives clients a level of comfort and trust in you (that you're in it for the long haul) and the industry.

> "...Doing voluntary work helps introduce you and your skills to the marketplace (although monitor this and don't be seen as an easy target for free work). Networking at events run by local groups, e.g. Chamber of Commerce, is time well spent. Listen to people and what they have to say ... they will soon ask what you do and that is your cue to tell them how you can possibly help them in their business."
> Faye Partridge, Partridge Typing & Print, Ltd.

One more important benefit to being a member of an industry association is to volunteer with them. This is a great way to meet other savvy entrepreneurs who share your goals and aspirations, and have a desire to make your industry stronger and more viable to potential clients.

This may mean allocating a few hours a week or month to volunteer on a committee, or agreeing to serve on a volunteer Board. All these activities will increase your exposure to others who understand the VA concept, and may require your particular product or service. It will also add polish to your bio and/or professional resume, which is key to being taken seriously in your chosen field.

Books

One of the least expensive training items you can buy for your business is books. Whether you need to learn about new marketing ideas, brush up on your writing skills or want to teach yourself all the advanced features of Excel, learning about these things can be as quick as a trip to your local (or online) bookstore or library. Read reviews of books online before you purchase to learn if the book is well-written and fulfills the objectives they are intended to.

Books allow you access to information any time you want it, allow you to easily refer to the information in the future and are relatively inexpensive.

The Web

While there is admittedly a lot of junk on the web, you can also find a lot of good information. Tons of free articles on the web are written by professionals in their fields. Go to sites like: (www.businessknowhow.com or www.inc.com) and do a search. These articles can help you learn a specific business skill or a complementary business skill like information on how to grow, run, or advertise your business.

In addition to static websites, you may find blogs on websites or podcasts in directories. These are a good way to get into the minds of professionals you want to be like or professionals you want to work with. Seek out people who are where you want to be and find out what they've done to get where they are. These more personal forms of communication can give you a good indicator.

Podcasts

Another relatively new form of information dissemination is the podcast. Podcasts are much like internet radio shows that cover all topics under the sun. They may range in length from five minutes to an hour. Like internet articles or website blogs, they can help you learn additional skills that will help your business.

Podcasts can be played through your computer or downloaded to a portable device like an iPod, which gives you some flexibility in your listening options. You can listen to a podcast in your car or while vacuuming or cutting the grass.

For a directory of podcasts, search for "podcast directories" or look for some of our specific resources at the end of the chapter.

Blogs

Blogs have gained in popularity over the past several years and offer a vast array of information and resources on just about every topic imaginable. Use bookmarking sites or simple search engine queries to find the top ranked blogs offering information about a specific topic of interest. You may even consider building relationships with some of the more popular blog owners who have a connection with your expertise. Exchanging articles on each other's blogs will help improve your expertise, and theirs.

> *"Belonging to professional organizations is very important to your growth and intra-industry exposure. It helps you develop relationships with peers who may offer advice, assistance and potential partnering opportunities. Volunteering affords the opportunity to brand yourself within your field and gives you the chance to share your personal experiences, show your ability to communicate and follow-through and lay the groundwork for other activities."*
> Sharon Williams, The 24-Hour Secretary

The Executive Summary

Working virtually doesn't have to mean "less skilled," but in this new and challenging industry, improving your Professional Development in any and all of the ways discussed earlier in this Chapter will help educate business professionals. Make professional development a priority in your business. Budget an amount that you devote to professional training and make sure you spend it.

When you make it a priority to keep up on new business technology, skills and marketing ideas, your business will benefit. Show your clients and yourself that you are worth the investment.

Chapter Links and Resources

Virtual Assistant & Business Training	www.assistu.com
	www.virtualbusinesstraining.com
	www.VAclassroom.com
	www.smallbizu.com
Certification Programs for VAs	www.ivaa.org
	http://vacertified.com
(Canada)	http://www.cvac.ca/Certification/CCVA.php
VA Associations & Organizations	www.ivaa.org
	www.allianceforvirtualbiz.com
	www.iava.org.uk (United Kingdom)
	www.vanetworking.com/
(UK)	www.virtual-offices.org.uk/
(Australia)	www.asecretary.com.au/
(Australia)	www.vadirectory.net
(Canada)	www.canadianva.net/
	www.nvas.org/

Specialty Association & Organizations

Real Estate	www.wcr.org
	www.realtor.org
	www.revanetwork.com
Canada Real Estate	www.crea.ca/
Accounting	http://aaahq.org/index.cfm
	www.aicpa.org/index.htm
	www.aswa.org/

Specialty Association & Organizations (continued)

	Author	www.virtualauthorsassistants.ning.com
	Coaches	www.wabccoaches.com/
		www.caspaa.com
	Speakers	www.nsaspeaker.org/
		www.executivespeakers.com/
	Australia Speakers	www.nationalspeakers.asn.au/
	IT	www.itaa.org/
	IT Canada	www.itac.ca/
Business Articles		www.businessknowhow.com
		www.sba.gov
		www.inc.com
		www.magportal.com
		www.findarticles.com/p/articles/tn_bus
		www.allbusiness.com
		www.Get-Articles.com
Podcast Resources		www.podcastalley.com
		www.juicereceiver.sourceforge.net/index.php
		www.apple.com/itunes/podcasts
		www.podcastbunker.com
Blog Resources		www.wordpress.com
		www.wordpress.org
		www.blogger.com
		www.typepad.com

Chapter Six

Marketing, Advertising & Public Relations

One question even veteran VAs asks each other is, "How do you market your business?" Marketing and advertising can be expensive and often deliver less-than-satisfactory results. Even successful VAs could probably tell you about at least one marketing failure they've experienced during their career.

In this chapter, you'll learn about some different options in getting your company's name in front of your target market. Some ideas are low-cost, some aren't, but the reality is that marketing and advertising is necessary for your business growth.

Marketing

No matter what type of business you're in, marketing is the key to your success. If no one knows your business exists, they can't hire you. Although Chapter Three on Branding is helpful in creating a marketable image, the way you bring your message to the marketplace can make or break your business.

> *"Word of mouth, first and foremost. My IVAA listing and association second, and participation in local networking events are the three best marketing tools I use."*
>
> Sandy Giusti, Consider it Done Virtual Assistant Services

In the beginning, at least twenty-five percent (25%) of your operating budget should be earmarked for marketing. Once you are more established, it should be twenty-five percent (25%) of your gross revenue in actual sales, or your targeted yearly sales.

Minimally you should be marketing your business 8-10 hours per week.

Effective marketing depends on many factors as it relates to your type of practice. It could mean paid ads, direct mail, or publicity.

Paid Advertising

Sometimes it makes sense to advertise in more traditional, general outlets. For example, if you specialize in medical transcription, then a properly categorized Yellow Pages listing, and some advertisements in trade magazines, would all be good expenditures in your marketing efforts.

Radio and Television ads will probably be too expensive for the average VA and would have too broad a demographic to be useful. But continually look for new advertising opportunities that would reach your target market. New developments in media offerings will surely bring about new opportunities for advertising. Some opportunities in the future might include advertising on internet radio, podcasts, or blogs. If you place an ad where your ideal audience will hear, see, or read it, it could be a good use of marketing dollars.

However, if your skills and specialty are focused on a particular market segment, like Realtors, you may find that paying the price for a Yellow Pages listing is less effective than taking those dollars to join or participate in Realtor associations, trade magazines, and online communities where real estate professionals would be hanging out.

Consider Bartering

Bartering your services may be a great way to get some upscale services, advertising options, or memberships for free (or at a reduced cost), to save on your marketing costs. However, bartering creates some tax implications, so be sure to discuss it with your CPA before considering this option.

How Do You Know What Works?

Unfortunately, there is no "magic bullet" when it comes to marketing. There are hundreds of ways to market your business and what works for one VA may not work for another. Take the time to attend some marketing classes or read books that are specifically about marketing, such as the *Guerilla Marketing Series* by Jay Conrad Levinson.

Not all of your marketing efforts will be successful. Some are just trial and error. You need to be consistent with your marketing and your message. It will take several "impressions" (statistics indicate 7-10 times) of your potential clients seeing or hearing your name before they will remember it. Use the same tagline, logo and message in all your materials.

Keep Track of Your Results

Make sure that you put features in place to monitor the success of each marketing option you implement. In other words, you need to have a good Return on Investment, or ROI. Some examples might include: offering the "first hour free" for mentioning this postcard, or 10% off your next three-hour minimum project offered only on an online listing, etc. If you're running advertising in a variety of places, offer a different promotional offer for each venue. Of course, always ask potential clients how they heard of you. Did they find you through a search engine and click through to your website? Did they see an article you wrote for an e-zine? Did they see an ad? If so, which one? Finding out will help you learn which of your marketing efforts are working and which you should scrap.

Keeping track of how effective each individual marketing plan works will help you to stretch your budget to get the biggest bang for your marketing bucks. As you begin to network with other businesspeople or VAs, ask them what works best in their practice...look for people who offer services, if you're selling services; and products, if you're selling products. Even though they may not be offering the same types of products or services, their insights will help you to decide what outlets may be good options to reach your target audience.

Word of Mouth Marketing

The absolute best marketing for any business is "word of mouth" marketing. This may come to you in a variety of ways. You can join a leads group such as BNI (Business Network International) that offers you the opportunity to be the ONLY person in your profession who is a part of that particular chapter. This gives you a distinct advantage because you will be the recipient of any referral business the members of your chapter may have, and you will not have to compete with anyone else offering the same types of products or services. This is a distinction you may not experience with a local Chamber or other business organization.

> *"[I get clients by] Word of mouth, and of course exceptional customer service, so they want to return – and tell their friends and associates!"*
>
> Marsha Wagner, CastleVisions

Referral business, (business that you get by asking a current client if they know of anyone that could use your products and/or services), is usually a great way to grow your practice. Businesspeople attract and associate with other businesspeople that think and act like they do. When your current clients give you referral business, you get a good, qualified lead that is already sold on your services and a great compliment to you and your talents. You can't ask for much more than that!

How to Get Free Publicity

Continuing to keep your name in the public eye will be instrumental in growing your business. Above and beyond your marketing and advertising budget, employ the use of publicity to get your name circulating. The best thing about publicity is much of it's free!

Any time you do something "new" or "achieve" something within your business, write a quick press release and submit it to your local newspapers, magazines, radio and TV stations, as well as through online PR services like PRWeb. Anything that's newsworthy would be of interest.

You may not consider the announcement of the creation of your business to be newsworthy, but, by submitting a press release, you get the "brand" of you out to those who can provide you with free publicity. Maybe ABC VA Practice isn't the most newsworthy press release you saw that day, but if you send it to someone who never heard of a VA, and thinks that the industry would be something of interest….guess who they'll call for more information?

What about that certification you achieved…or your volunteer position serving on a local or online Board of Directors? These are all opportunities to create a press release and submit it to your contacts. You may not get published immediately, but with perseverance, and some good writing skills, you will eventually get a return on your investment—which is usually only time.

Even better, tie your business to something going on in the news. News editors are always looking for new and interesting twists to current events. For example, if a new statistic gets published about how much time the average employee "wastes" on the job, you can write a press release about it and educate their readers that hiring a VA saves businesses money because they're only paying for "productive" time. When you can tie your business to something newsworthy, you drastically raise your odds of getting coverage.

> "I believe a great part of my success when I was first starting out was my willingness to 'work' 40 hours a week, even though I didn't have 40 hours worth of client work. I still 'went to work' every morning and put in a full day. During that time, if I didn't have client work, then I worked my marketing, developing forms and procedures, and learning new skills."
>
> Barbie Dallmann, Happy Fingers Word Processing & Business Services

Other ways to take advantage of free publicity include writing articles for local business magazines, newspapers, free article sites, or online forums or blogs. Perhaps you can participate in an association's newsletter. Even better, agree to donate your time to organize and create their newsletter. Ask if they'd be willing to credit your efforts in the newsletter by including your business card-sized ad. These are all examples of ways to communicate and present your talents to others who may have a need for your product or service. Be sure to look for something that is a good "fit" for the products and/or services you provide. If you're not looking for newsletter business, that's probably not a good fit for you. If you're looking to attract web design clients, writing articles about the advantages or pros and cons of the different types of websites is the way to go. Or volunteer to design your association's website.

Bottom line, all of these options offer you the opportunity to include your bio, contact information and resources to connect readers to you and/or your website to get more information about how they can work with you, this wonderfully, talented, expert who is published in multiple arenas.

You can also get free publicity by offering to speak at local business meetings, like the Rotary Club, Kiwanis Club, Women's Council of Realtors, trade shows, educational seminars, etc., especially those places that will "advertise" or list your speaking engagement in local and/or online venues. This is a great way to get your message out to other businesspeople, and perhaps even your target market, plus, you have the added benefit of getting public speaking experience. If you ever decide to become a consultant, serve on Boards of Directors, or do trainings as your business matures, you'll be glad you feel comfortable speaking in front of a crowd.

Sales

I'm sure you're thinking, four-letter word when we mention, 'sales', but you will need to have or develop sales skills to grow your business. All the best, most creative marketing in the world won't close the sale. You will have to do that! But don't let that word scare you off. In the past few chapters, we've been setting up and developing your sales strategy without you even knowing it.

Many people believe that you have to be aggressive, and posses the, used car salesmen gene in order to succeed in sales. Nothing could be further from the truth. The most successful salespeople have two valuable skills. They're good listeners, and they make their pitch all about the client's pain, or problem, and communicate how they can solve it. The prospects actually sell themselves in this model, and what could be better than that?

Just as we encouraged you not to make your 60-second infomercial a laundry list of your products and services, the sales call, or closing the sale shouldn't be either. Don't expend a lot of your time touting how great you are, your software proficiency, or all the in-depth information you include in your seminar. It's not about you, it's about them.

Whether by telephone, electronically, or in person, ask them a series of questions that will alert you to their problem or need, and what aspect of that problem is most important to them. This will give you insight into what additional questions might lead you to provide a solution that matches the need, and relieves their pain. By this point in the conversation, they are getting ready to close the sale for themselves, and will decide that you are the perfect provider. You immediately communicated that you care about them, and are more concerned about their need than you are about stopping by to peddle your products or services.

This simple process also allows you to decide whether or not this potential client is a good fit for you, fits into your "A" or "B" client criteria, and has the ability to be a long-term, or short-term client. It also allows you to control the conversation, so that you can steer them to the logical conclusion, you're the only person who understands them and can take their pain away.

Will there be bloody noses? Absolutely. Will those situations teach you how to do it better the next time? You bet! We're not ever going to close every sale, not even the BEST salespeople will. But taking a positive approach, and never being afraid to try again, will most assuredly result in more closes than rejections. And every time you repeat the process the easier it becomes.

So don't be afraid of the "S" word, consider it one more opportunity to find out what's needed in the marketplace and learn to see where you fit into the mix.

Giveaways

Promotional products with your name and logo on them are a great way to get your message out, at a minimal cost. Work with a professional promotional products company so that they can help you with ideas that will work within your budget, and still reach the audience that will best serve your needs.

Of course, you can always offer "gift certificates" for your products or services as a way to attract a new client, or one that's on the fence—who's not sure if they should, or could use your services. Although this may not attract the "right" client for you, it is another way to get your message out to someone who may not have been aware of what you have to offer. Be sure to write "Transferable" on the gift certificate. If the person you sent it to doesn't need it, she might know the perfect person who could use a VA.

Social Media & Bookmarking

In mid to late 2006, social media and social bookmarking came onto the scene. While most of us were still grasping the advantages of podcasting, this opportunity began to gain momentum.

A study conducted in March 2009 by Michael A. Stelzner took a look at how marketers are using social media to grow their businesses. Along with some interesting statistics, several things came to the forefront that would be beneficial to growing a small or home-based business.

Most people were only utilizing social media marketing for several months, and used it for an average of five hours per week, with the top benefit being business exposure, increased Internet traffic, and building new business relationships. The top tools in order of importance were, Twitter, blogs, LinkedIn and Facebook. With that in mind, we have spent this past year focusing on these four platforms, not only to promote our own businesses, but to develop a new service to provide to our clientele.

The first thing to consider is the low to no-cost benefits of utilizing this type of marketing strategy. Some of the costs you may incur would include, but are not limited to: purchasing a domain and hosting it for a blog; and blog themes (there are plenty of free ones out there, but sometimes you have a need that only a specific theme can support). The Twitter-sphere has grown by leaps and bounds with a long list of tools and add-ons that allow you to take the original intent of Twitter and expand it into a more business-minded focus.

> "In the beginning I relied far more heavily on my professional associations. Now, if I have a specific question, for instance, if I need to know what vendor to go to for a particular task, I'll ask colleagues in the IVAA. I can also say the IVAA RFP system is wonderful!"
>
> Jackie Eastwick, Allison Lane Business Solutions

LinkedIn, with its groups and 'answers' options truly keyed in on the small to medium-sized business marketer, although we are seeing more larger corporations diving into this aspect of social media marketing.

Facebook, originally considered to be a spin-off of MySpace (it was determined that MySpace was geared more towards teenagers, making Facebook a more adult-based atmosphere.) has been shown to attract mostly women in the 45-57 age group. Indications as of December 2009 were that Facebook was slow to respond to the needs created through the popularity of Twitter, and although their 'fan pages' and recent group options have begun to level the playing field, they still need to respond to the other benefits entrepreneurs are finding on other platforms.

Social bookmarking sites, touted as the next BIG thing, have started to take shape as an opportunity to promote video and audio in a somewhat similar fashion, and increased popularity of sites such as YouTube and Vimeo.

So how and why should you consider social media as a part of your overall business marketing plan? Simply, because it's so hot, and because it's relatively 'free.' Let's begin with a look at how it all works.

Social media sites such as Twitter, Facebook, LinkedIn, and Plaxo allow you to post brief messages (some, like Twitter, at a maximum of 140 characters) to capture the attention of your friends, family, or target market. If at all possible, you may want to consider having a separate 'personal' social media account where you will only attract friends and family, however, you can still successfully manage a business profile including your friends and family, and providing them updates (posts) that include both personal and business-related information.

> *"My clients are my greatest salespeople. 99.5% of the time, my new clients come from current or previous clients. I also utilize my networking group memberships. I do not advertise anywhere, nor will I. Referrals based on relationships are the way to go."*
>
> Sue Kramer, Peace of Mind Virtual Assistance

Why does social media help you increase your success online? Let's begin by discussing a post to your blog. Posts should be about 200-300 words, and give enough information so that people will get a feel for your expertise, and value. These should NOT be salesy messages, or spammy. That's absolutely not how this works. Though you will be able to do some sales messages, they are only a small portion of your social media image.

You will post your message to your blog. And though people can sign up on your blog for an RSS feed (Really Simple Syndication – a feed reader or aggregator), which will notify them that you've made a post to your blog, you still will want to announce your latest post and connect people, through social media, to your blog.

One of the main reasons is because the search engines look at blogs and blog platforms a little differently. Because of the interaction of the comments, the ability for the lay person to add and update the blog effectively, and the open source of blog platforms (our favorite is WordPress.org, others to consider would be TypePad or Blogger - from Google), as the content and information spiders out to the Web, it gives consistent attention to your blog, and website (which should be linked from your blog), and this attention translates into increased search engine optimization (SEO).

That being said, this is based upon our suggested practice of posting to your blog at least once a week. This is much easier to handle and not as hard to manage as a static website, which you probably only update about once a quarter, if not less. By utilizing a blog, search engines take note of the more regular activities and increase your rankings based upon this newfound popularity.

You may want to consider WordPress.org and host a domain that either links back to your main website URL – so www.mybusiness.com/blog, or a brand new URL like, www.mybusinessblog.com, rather than utilize WordPress.com (which is really for personal blogs, not business), or some other service that creates a URL like, www.wordpress.com/mycompanyblog, etc., which does not put your most professional foot forward.

Now that you've posted to the blog, you need to attract your target market to the blog so that they obtain the knowledge and resources you're sharing, which create your expert status, and bring attention to your offerings. This is where Twitter, Facebook, and LinkedIn come into play. By posting a brief 'teaser' message to your Twitter, Facebook, and LinkedIn platforms, including a link to the post on your blog, you draw attention to your materials and allow for a larger following.

Better yet, if someone on your contact list finds this information especially interesting, they can re-Tweet, or share it with their entire contact list, which expands your reach even further. This is not a bad thing at all. Each week as you post to your blog and connect people to it through your other social media, you will see a significant increase in the number of people who will now follow you.

Initially, it was thought that you should 'follow' or connect with anyone who connected to you. We believe that you should be more focused on your target market, and make sure that the types of people you are connecting to are a good match for you personally, or professionally. It hasn't taken long for spammers and pornographers to find their way to social media, and this could immediately tarnish your business reputation, so be focused on who you connect to, and add to your contacts.

To increase your followers, you will want to include some search options to find those people who have a need for your product or service. Each platform has different options for increasing your contacts and exposing larger numbers of prospects to your resources and information. Social media allows you to build relationships with people who may become clients, or lead you to prospective clients because of their sphere of influence.

People do business with you because they know, like, and trust you. Social media can provide a global opportunity to build a following more quickly than any other marketing option we've considered.

This is why your posts should be mostly informational and provide resources, instead of trying to sell your services; it's a vehicle to use to begin to develop a relationship that will lead the prospect to know, like, and trust you, thereby opening the door for you to do business together.

Here are a few key elements to use when trying to capture your target market on social media. For Twitter, try the following options to look for people who would fit your business:

- Search.twitter.com
- Twibes.com
- Twello.com
- Twittergrader.com
- Twinfluence.com
- Tweetcloud.com

Once you find groups of people, click on their profile photos and begin to 'follow' them. Another great way to piggy-back on someone else's followers is to join larger groups that would have people in your target market.

So if your target market is REALTORS or coaches, search for those groups and you'll be able to follow a more targeted group of prospects who would be interested to hear from you and benefit from your information and resources.

Facebook allows you to click on a person's contacts (left side toolbar), with the click of a few buttons. Let's say your target market is attorneys, and you have a CPA as one of your followers. Because many attorneys also have connections to CPAs, by looking at 'everyone' on their friends list, you are able to click on their contacts and find the CPAs among them who you may want to connect with.

This is a great way to expand your contacts in a very focused way. You can also 'search' for types of groups, but at this time, Facebook is not as focused on groups as LinkedIn is.

LinkedIn is all about business. In the simple search dropdown menu, you can search for specific people, groups, companies, answers, or jobs. You will want to key in on groups that fit your professional life. So while you will want to connect with virtual assistance groups to stay on top of industry news, resources and technology, you can also connect with your target market by utilizing LinkedIn groups.

Once you have joined a group, you are able to post a tidbit of your information and a link to the blog post, again, to increase your SEO and build your database of prospects. This option allows you to connect to thousands of people in your target market who may not already be connected to you and your contact list. You will find this to be a vital part of your social media marketing plan because of your ability to clearly target your message to people who will benefit from what you have to offer.

You will also want to periodically check the 'answers' section (located in the upper toolbar) of LinkedIn to answer any questions that someone may have asked to the entire LinkedIn community – this puts your expertise and information out in front of millions, yes, millions of people who could benefit from what you have to offer. This is HUGE.

You may want to set aside at least 30 minutes each week, as a part of your normal marketing plan, to answer questions and increase your exposure.

Probably the most difficult part of utilizing social media marketing in your overall marketing plan is the time needed to pull this all together. While it may seem overwhelming, once you set the initial setup in motion, you can easily expand your plan to include a specific amount of time each day or week to market your business through these Internet-based options.

Before we get any farther along, you also want to be sure to spend a good amount of your initial setup time in creating a really great profile. Your photo is an absolute must. Since you do have a global reach, and you may not ever personally meet many of your prospects or clients, having a face to add to the name and expertise is vital.

Each platform allows you different profile aspects. Make sure that you put your best foot forward and give an overview (not a laundry list of your services) of 'what's in it for them' when modifying your profile details. You will most assuredly want to include links back to your main static website, as well as your blog, and have links to social media (as of this writing, some sites are offering direct links in your profile section to other social media platforms – we presume this will be universal someday soon).

When someone reads a post they find interesting or beneficial, the next thing they will do is look at your profile. In your LinkedIn account, you can even connect to your current clients (which we highly recommend), and ask them to craft a recommendation for you. This increases the potential for a prospect to choose you over another competitor, as it's always more beneficial to relate to someone who has used your services, than it is for someone to work with you simply because YOU told them you're their best option.

Please note that you should always keep an independent file of any of your LinkedIn recommendations. If for some reason someone recommends you and then deletes their LinkedIn account, that recommendation could be lost forever. You will also want to utilize these recommendations on other sites (like a testimonials page on your website), and in other venues, like your blog, sales pages, and/or email marketing or eZine software like Constant Contact, Swift Page, Exact Target, etc.

Social Bookmarking is touted to be the NEXT big thing in the social media arena. Bookmarking sites are a little different, they are not focused on people following or being a friend to you, but a way for you to post details/teasers to your blog posts, products/services, videos, and common interest information that helps people get a better sense of who you are and what your likes and dislikes are on both a personal and professional level.

Some of the most popular sites are:

- Delicious.com
- Digg.com
- StumbleUpon.com
- Technorati.com

Create accounts in two or three of them and play around to see what's available. Because they are just coming of age, they are not as focused on creating a following and getting your message out to a larger market, but they do have their place in the overall marketing of any small to medium-sized business. You may want to use these sites to search for other experts in your field to see what they're doing to attract a larger target audience. They are also a good option for anyone who is using video as a part of their marketing plan.

Let's take a few moments to discuss how we can incorporate all that we've learned about social media into a balanced marketing plan. First, we need to discuss how you will market yourself at each level of social media.

You may find an 80/20 plan to be the best, meaning that 80% of your posts are either personal, fun, informational, or provide resources; and 20% of your posts create an urgency to 'buy from you', whether it be a physical product, or a service.

Going back to the know-like-trust factor, using this 80/20 plan will allow you to focus more on what's in it for the prospect, than just trying to close a sale. Social media is a great way to build relationships on any level (personal or professional) that will lead to business growth within a few short months.

Make sure your information and resources are relevant, and put you in the best possible light to prospects, clients, and even friends and family. You may need to make messages from your cranky uncle 'private' so as not to let anyone else see unsavory posts from any of your contacts, but it is possible to maintain the highest caliber of contact/follower, without taking a hit to your reputation. Check out all the tools and options before you accept anyone into your contact sphere, these are important 'first steps' in making a successful social media marketing plan.

You may find that you get the most attention (comments/replies) to some of your personal posts. It allows people to see another side of you, outside of your business persona. So if you're an avid gardener in addition to being an entrepreneur, you will connect on a different level to a larger group of people if several times a week you discuss some of your love for gardening.

Something as simple as, "Saw a beautiful Monarch butterfly as I watered my container garden today.", or "My herbs are going great this season.", can really attract attention, and the more attention you draw, the more people who will follow you and begin to see your benefit and value.

You may also want to connect people to other news reports and information that are of interest to you. Let's say you're a star-gazer and you read an online news article about a meteor shower happening in a few days. Posting a link to this article along with a brief message, like 'Might be a great show in the night sky on Wednesday" will attract a lot of attention to you, and because this interests a broader audience, you will most likely see additional hits to your site.

To get a better idea of what I mean, you may want to use a technology called bit.ly for creating shorter links to your blog posts or other news articles. Bit.ly allows you to track the hits to the URL's you create. For example, you may find that you had 65 hits of 8,145 views of a particular post – how could this happen.

Well, this means that 65 people on your social media (people who are currently following you) clicked on your link and read your post. They found it so compelling some of them re-Tweeted, or forwarded your post to THEIR list of contacts. Can you see how this immediately expands your reach and how those 65 followers spread the word, and maybe some of those people spread the word to their list, and so on, allowing you to reach a much larger market that you'd ever imagined? Bit.ly is a great tool to allow you to track your links.

Understanding this feature will help you to create better posts and more compelling headlines that yield far-reaching and increased results. What you will find happening is that after you've attracted the attention of all these additional contact groups, you'll get a surge of new followers and requests to connect.

Just be sure that you look closely at their profiles to make sure you are connecting with the right people for your specific personal and professional needs. Especially with Twitter, if you are asked to connect with someone without a photo, or without a bio, be very wary. These are most likely not going to be the best people for your contact sphere.

Once you get the hang of it, the next thing you'll want to be aware of, is how easily time can get away from you. This type of marketing is much more 'fun' than traditional marketing and it's very easy to expend way more time than you had imagined.

One of the best ways to keep things flowing properly and not create overwhelm is to allow yourself a specific amount of time each day, or week, to focus on this marketing medium. Perhaps 30 minutes a day, or 4 hours a week; whatever works best for you. Once you establish the amount of time you're looking to expend on this medium, find a way to make yourself accountable to stay within those parameters. You might use a simple kitchen timer, or an Outlook reminder to keep you aware of the time you're spending in each platform.

You can also use some technologies that allow you to schedule posts, or post to multiple sites at one time. Our favorites include:

- Ping.fm
- Onlywire.com
- Tweetlater.com
- HootSuite.com

Creating a simple program of posting to your blog at least once a week, and other social media, like Facebook, LinkedIn, and Twitter at least once a day or minimally three times a week, will allow you to open you to increased prospects and clients. We do not suggest that you use ONLY social media as your marking program, but it can and should be 40-50% of your overall marketing program.

In addition, once you have a good feel for working in social media, you can add this to your list of client services. Social Media Marketing is HOT, and it's a great way to support your current clients on a much larger scale, while opening doors you may not have been able to open in the past to a new breed of clientele. Most entrepreneurs know they need to be involved with social media, they simply don't know where to start, or how they'll find the time. This creates a way to expand into a new market share and increase your expertise.

Social media marketing and bookmarking will continue to grow and expand faster than you can imagine, and certainly more quickly than we're able to publish additions to this book. Take some time to establish yourself on three to four of the options mentioned here, and watch as your business takes on a new level of exposure, increases your Internet traffic, builds new partnerships, and grows your SEO.

The Executive Summary

The biggest concept you should embrace for your advertising, marketing, and public relations efforts is remembering to ask yourself this question: "Is this message going to reach my target audience?" Does it speak to their 'pain', the problem that working with you will solve?" If the answer is no, don't spend the money. Marketing your practice effectively is really about being a 'problem solver'....their problem creates the need for your products and services. Make sure the message effectively answers their question, "What's in it for me?".

You'll probably find that, in the beginning, you'll make some "mistakes" spending your marketing budget. That's okay, just about everyone has. But don't be paralyzed by second-guessing yourself. Know what your advertising/marketing/PR budget is and make sure you don't skimp on this area of your business...spend that time and money every month. Even for PR activities, you may not be spending (much) money, but you are investing your time, so make sure you also get a good return on your time invested.

As time goes on and you can quantify your ROI, you'll begin to know which of your expenditures gives you the most bang for your buck and you'll be able to hone in your marketing efforts for maximum impact with your target market.

> *"Hiring staff and learning to manage and delegate responsibilities is a challenge for someone who begins with a one-person shop, but it's one of the best moves I made in growing the business."*
> Vicki L. Duncan, Duncan Business Services, Inc.

Here are some marketing and advertising ideas to consider (Some online options are detailed at the end of this Chapter):

- Local free papers
- Yellow pages ads
- Online websites your potential clients visit
- Postcards
- Press releases
- Promotional articles
- Blogs
- Podcasts
- Online communities
- Online associations and business listings
- Gift certificates
- Trade or industry magazine ads
- Social Media Marketing

Recommended reading for marketing ideas:

"The Purple Cow" by Seth Godin

"Guerilla Marketing" Series, by Jay Conrad Levinson

Chapter Links and Resources

Business Network International (BNI)	www.bni.com
Chamber resources	www.uschamber.com
	www.chamberofcommerce.com
	www.nationalbcc.org
	www.thewomenschamber.com
	www.2chambers.com/
Online PR Resources	www.prweb.com
	www.prfree.com

Online PR Resources (cont.)	www.online-pr.com
	www.pressbox.co.uk/
	www.webwire.com
Publish Articles Online	editor@saintrochtree.com
	freecontent@yahoogroups.com
	newsletter@webpromote.com
	publishyours@onelist.com
Free Article Submission Sites	www.ezinearticles.com
	www.selfgrowth.com
	www.about.com
	www.amazines.com
	www.articlealley.com
	www.articledashboard.com
	www.articlefeeder.com
	www.articlehub.com
	www.articleson.com
	www.constantcontent.com
	www.ezinearticledirectory.com
	www.goarticles.com
	www.ideamarketers.com
	www.searchwarp.com
	www.ultimatearticledirectory.com
Civic Groups	www.rotary.org
	www.kiwanis.org
	www.wcr.org
	www.optimist.org

Promotional Products	www.ppa.org
	www.promomart.com
	www.cafepress.com
	www.ppam.org
Social Media Marketing Resources	www.search.twitter.com
	www.Twibes.com
	www.Twello.com
	www.Twittergrader.com
	www.Twinfluence.com
	www.Tweetcloud.com
	www.Delicious.com
	www.Digg.com
	www.StumbleUpon.com
	www.Technorati.com
	www.Ping.fm
	www.Onlywire.com
	www.Tweetlater.com
	www.HootSuite.com

Free Blog Themes

http://www.wpspider.com/category/home-and-furniture-free-wordpress-layouts/

http://topwpthemes.com/

www.wordpress.org/extend/themes

Also know there are premium themes that you can pay for. Most are inexpensive, $60 - $80. We like themes from www.ithemes.com, www.studiopress.com, www.woothemes.com

Chapter Seven

The Challenges of Working From Home

*B*eing your own boss and working virtually comes with many challenges. Some of these include: isolation, learning to build relationships with people "virtually," and maintaining the delicate balance between work, play, and family.

Even though these challenges can seem overwhelming at times, you will find that having your own business and working virtually have enormous "pros" that will far outweigh the "cons."

To truly enjoy the success of any business, remind yourself to find ways to leave the work behind and enjoy the life you're hoping to support through the labor of love you now know as your VA practice.

Balancing Work and Home

Whether your business is home-based or functions from leased or owned office space, finding the right balance between work, play, and family can be a challenge for any business owner, but one that you can easily learn to manage with minimal stress. Although being your own boss allows you many freedoms, having a good time management system in place will be an important tool in balancing work, play, and home.

> *"The best way I've found to balance work and home is to maintain regular office hours. I don't allow work to intrude on my off-time. Likewise, I don't attempt to do things like laundry or housecleaning during the workday."*
>
> Heather Lee, design/type

Scheduling and Boundaries

You may find that it makes sense to organize appointments and personal schedules in separate systems. Perhaps two online or hardcopy calendars will work best, or maybe one system either online, hardcopy or both, to keep business and personal schedules under control. You may find that you prefer to keep everything on your computer in Outlook, for example, or you may prefer a week-at-a-glance paper appointment book. Try a few different styles of appointment management until you find something that's perfect for you.

Especially for those who are home-based, you will deal with additional interruptions that you may not have considered. You will most likely find that you don't know how anything ever got done at your home when you were working for someone else. You may suddenly find that you will need to allow a few hours a week to handle home repairs and maintenance. If you do, realize that just because you may have 40 hours available to work doesn't mean you'll want to (or be able to) work on client projects that whole time.

> "I personally enjoy working AND playing hard. Although I am putting in countless dedicated hours to my business, I am aware of the times that I need to get away from my office and computer for a break. I enjoy various hobbies, traveling and other activities that are completely separate from my work world, which definitely help me stay in balance. Staying RESTED is also an important piece of the puzzle!"
> Lisa Hoffman, Premier Administrative Services

Try scheduling out-of-office trips so that you can also accommodate running a few errands as well as picking up client print shop projects, getting your mail, or making deposits at the bank. (Don't forget to write-off your work-related mileage!) The enemy of a VA is unstructured time. If you find yourself regularly taking in a movie during a workday, going shopping or taking long lunches, your business will suffer. By now, you should know how many billable hours you need to complete in a week to meet your expenses, and income/sales goals.

Once your business is thriving, maintain reasonable, attainable goals in scheduling and accepting client project deadlines. Don't get in the habit of taking on so many projects with such short deadlines that there is no way you can keep up and do anything outside of work. If you do, you'll regret it and stand to tarnish your reputation with clients. No one wants to work with someone who cannot meet their promised deadlines!

You may be tempted to reorganize your life by failing to get out with friends or spending less time with family in order to grow your practice. Although you will definitely be making some sacrifices initially, doing your best to make sure you schedule personal and family time will go far in keeping stress levels to a minimum.

Having your own business doesn't mean that you have to put your personal life on hold. You will have to plan on spending some of your evenings trying out different forms of networking, attending classes, or working on your marketing efforts. Doing so allows you to spend your day meeting with potential clients, and achieving client project deadlines, but finding time for family and friends is vital to maintaining your sanity. Make sure to schedule some social outings with friends and family, too.

Be prepared to set boundaries with family and friends who may be more demanding because they think that now that you work from home, you have all sorts of time on your hands. Help them understand that you are serious about growing a successful business, and not just sitting at home, eating bon-bons, watching the soaps, or waiting for them to call and gab. Caller ID is a great investment for your personal and business phone lines. When friends call, let it go to voice mail and call them back at your convenience.

Discourage friendly visits during the workday. If someone wants to stop by and see you, set expectations early. Say something like, "I'd love for you to drop by and pick up that book I promised you. But I'm really busy with work, so I'll only be able to chat for about ten minutes." Then stick to that deadline. Be polite, but firm. You need to "train" people to respect your time.

Consider that your family and friends could also be a good source of potential clients, if you can help them to understand what you do, and how you can help people increase their productivity. It's important to maintain good open communication and look to each other as a source of support and guidance. They may also have need of your services. Leave no stone unturned. You may find your next $1000 a month client standing in line at the grocery store.

Another time stealer can be your self-esteem. Playing the role of sales manager and salesperson may require going outside of your comfort zone. Working from home can give you a houseful of excuses for not making those cold calls, attending that online business class, or local business luncheon to market your business. Be reasonable with yourself, and force yourself to think outside the box and take action.

Although it is great to be at home where you can throw in a load of laundry, clean the house, or run personal errands, do so within reason, and make sure you're not avoiding tasks important to the growth of your business or those things you are not comfortable handling. If at all possible, outsource some of those tasks, like lawn care and house cleaning, to allow as much time as possible for running your business.

"Balancing workload and home life is tricky. I rarely charge for my time after the close of the business day, but find that other work-related issues, such as billing, volunteering, website development, writing proposals, etc., get squeezed into my off hours and encroach on my family time."
Caroline Wright, The Wright Solution

Handling Isolation

Even if you have employees, running your own business means you may find yourself more isolated than when you worked in the corporate arena. For those working solo, isolation can come in many forms. You may wish you could chat around the water cooler about last night's sitcom episode, or feel sad you have no one to share lunch with. The isolation of working alone can be challenging for the social creature in all of us. There are others who actually enjoy the isolation and tout it as a benefit of having their own business. As long as it's 'healthy' and you're not limiting your growth by being a hermit, enjoy the peace and tranquility that isolation may afford you.

Attending local networking events and making time to meet with business associates can help resolve some feelings of isolation. Get involved in online industry-related associations or online business forums where you can meet peers and other business people who have your same interests and aspirations. Join chat sessions or attend online business seminars to increase your knowledge and your customer database. The list of possibilities is endless. Find something that feels right and fits into your schedule.

> "It's different than working a full-time job because your office is calling to you from the other room."
> Kimberley Thomas-Catanzaro, Bookkeeping & Secretarial Services

Don't let the isolation bring you down or lower your spirits. Remember this is a normal part of starting a small business and common to most VAs. Use the isolation as your motivation to get out there and meet new people who share the same issues and are willing to help you focus on more positive aspects of operating your practice.

You may also find that you need to sever some old relationships with friends or peers that no longer have synergy with your new goals and aspirations. Surrounding yourself with more positive and optimistic people will help you to stay on track and keep you inspired to work through the challenges that you now face.

As an entrepreneur, you will need to develop a "new attitude" as it relates to your image and those whose company you keep. Remember that everyone you associate with will help to develop the image of your company. Make sure that you are always ready to put your best and most professional foot forward. These new relationships and the changes in your old ones will help you handle the drawbacks of the isolation of being a sole practitioner.

If you find you still have feelings of isolation, try volunteering your time in any number of ways. Whether it's a few hours a week for an industry association, volunteering to do the monthly newsletter for a local Chamber, offering to speak at a Rotary meeting, writing articles for a local business newspaper or ezine, or giving a few hours at the local school or hospital, it will translate into "free" publicity for you and your company.

Working virtually can and will create feelings of isolation. As your business becomes more successful, you will, at times, long for a little isolation to recharge your batteries, and then there will be times when you hunger to build relationships you already have. You may also look for new contacts to make sure that you will have someone to bounce ideas off of, and be able to call on them whenever the need arises. It will be your personal choice to find the combination that is the right fit for you.

> *"I enjoy working virtually so I don't feel isolated very often and I have a lot of contact via email and usually feel like people are right there for me."*
> Janice Wlodarski,
> Professional Publishing Services

Handling Small Children

For many, the allure of working from home stems from a desire to provide full-time childcare while still bringing in a sustainable income. While a home-based business could be the perfect way to accomplish those goals, it is still wise to set and maintain ground rules for your business and your children.

Most children, especially in their younger years, need structure. Having and maintaining specific structure to your business is just as important. This may translate into scheduled childcare certain days or times throughout the week. Not only does this help maintain your focus on the business, but gives younger children the structure they need and the social interaction with other children their age that is important to their development. Having specific times designated as "business time" or "family time" is important to the well-being of yourself, your clients, and your children.

When younger children who do not attend school full-time are a part of your routine, you may find child rearing overwhelming when you add the demands of a small business. Especially if you are the main caregiver to the children after-hours, you may also feel as if you haven't spoken to an adult in months. This is why it's so important to make time for some adult play in your life. Whether it's making sure that you have a date night scheduled with your significant other once every two weeks, or planning for a girls' or guys' night out, keeping some play dates of your own will go far in keeping balance in your life.

This scenario also presents many challenges when you're trying to build a business and need to get out there and network, or attend classes. Make sure that you have daycare and sitter options in place that can address the needs of your business. Likewise, make it clear to clients your availabilities to work on projects, or other business needs they may have, as it relates to the needs of your children.

Home workers are much more prevalent in this day and age, so clients will understand your need to set and maintain these boundaries. It's always best to be honest and upfront with your clients. It helps build trust; an important factor in building strong relationships with them.

The good news is that you are not alone. Many VAs have thriving practices and enjoy the benefits and rewards of owning their own business and raising their children. Finding VAs that share your business style and focus will help you to gain knowledge and support to help you handle any of the challenges you face as a home worker.

The Executive Summary

Finding the right balance between work, play and family is most likely the hardest of our "virtual" challenges, but one that can easily be managed with minimal stress. Remember, this is your business; you make the rules. Stay positive; set-up a working appointment and/or calendar system; make sure that you don't take on extra responsibilities or use home chores to "avoid" marketing your business; and set reasonable boundaries for yourself, family, friends and clients to help keep your business and personal lives in balance.

The key to enjoying working from home and running a successful business is to become efficient with your time. Make sure you get out of your house occasionally.

Make sure you have provisions made for small children so you have some uninterrupted time to work and go to networking events. This allows them to get the socialization and structure they need and allows you time to focus on your business without distraction.

> "My website is currently my main source of business."
> Nina Feldman,
> Nina Feldman Connections

Running your own virtual assistant business can be very rewarding. While the biggest hazard is feeling isolated, by planning your family, business and play time, you can find the right mix you need to enjoy the balance and success you've been searching for.

Chapter Links and Resources

Online Calendars/
Appointment Scheduling

www.calendar.yahoo.com

www.calendarzone.com

www.airset.com

www.calendar.google.com

Chapter Eight

Ethical Considerations

*E*thics plays a big part in your success. Having a good Code of Ethics, or having ethical business practices in place, will communicate to clients that they are dealing with a professional they can trust with their confidential company information and documents.

Clients need to feel that they are working with someone who understands the importance of keeping proprietary information confidential. Make sure that you have a strong, viable, and ethical business practice that will make it over the long haul. You also need to surround yourself with organizations, associations and vendors that share the same level of ethical standards as your own.

> *"Always have high integrity, honesty, and a great work ethic and you'll get a great reputation. The VA industry is a very small world and reputations travel."*
>
> Sue Kramer, Peace of Mind Virtual Assistance

Another important aspect in touting your ethical practices is to seek out certification and designations, such as the EthicsCheck™ designation available through the International Virtual Assistants Association (www.ivaa.org).

Having and maintaining ethical business practices helps clients and vendors feel comfortable working together with the knowledge that they are going to be treated fairly in all aspects of their business and personal relationships with you. Even more important than your talents and skills, business ethics is the backbone of a healthy, stable business, allowing you to communicate the true value you bring to the relationship and partnership between the two organizations.

By simply saying, "no" to an overly demanding client who requests an unrealistic deadline or discount, or being totally honest about your level of proficiency or knowledge of the software needed for a client project, your commitment to business ethics will be evident to clients, vendors, family, friends, and peers. Differentiate yourself from others who may not take the time or understand the benefits of implementing good ethical standards. It's a great investment in the health and well-being of your practice.

Accurately Representing your Experience and Capabilities

Your willingness to communicate honestly with clients, vendors and associates has a long-lasting impact on these relationships. Imagine how much more willing you would be to continue to do business with a client who calls you to tell you that you forgot to invoice them for something. Tell a client that you could refer them to someone with more expertise in a specific task, and that client is sure to call you whenever they have a need. Having good ethical skills will allow you to get to the next level with your clients.

In many cases, new clients choose to start with smaller, less involved "test" projects in order to build their confidence in your abilities and business practices. This is your opportunity to start building a long-term relationship that can evolve into more business, and more referrals, which are the best compliments a client can give you.

Misrepresenting your talents and skills tells clients that you are desperate and feel you need to cheat to win, or you need the business so badly that you would lie to get it. This is not the message you want to send, and not one that's going to encourage clients to call you for future projects. Asking peers or clients what software and training you would need to complete a particular task is seen as trying to be something you're not, and could cause irreparable damage to your reputation, as well as your company's. You won't stay in business long by behaving in this manner.

That's not to say that you can't research and consider expanding your practice to include more skills and client options, but make sure that you don't try and take a 'crash course' to be able to complete a client request. They will respect you more by being upfront and honest, and giving them the option of having you connect them with someone who has the experience and skills needed to produce a quality work product, offer to coordinate this task with someone else for them, or let them know you'd be willing to take the time to get the experience and skills to produce the quality results they deserve. This will go a long way in communicating to the client that you have their best interests at heart, and not just your own.

Our ethical standards have a direct relationship to our self-esteem, and by accepting our limits and abilities, we communicate that we feel confident in ourselves and our services, and that they are a valuable asset to our clients. We don't have to take on work that doesn't fit our skill-set because we know that there's plenty of business out there fitting our expertise. By honestly representing our skills, our clients will be satisfied and will tell others about having had a pleasant experience that allowed them to concentrate on functions that help them generate and increase their income and profit.

Keeping Client Files Safe

A vital part of your business relationships will consist of creating, maintaining, and storing client files. It's important that everyone understands and feels confident that you have security and storage systems in place to protect their data, and keep it available when they need it.

Accepting responsibility for having and keeping client files available can be a real lifesaver to a client whose system crashes, or who may accidentally damage the original file. This continues to solidify your relationship with clients, vendors, and peers. Now, instead of just providing them with services, you're also giving them peace of mind.

Consider having detailed guidelines in place so that clients know what measures you take to protect them, and so it allows you to differentiate yourself from competitors. Include information in your Work for Hire Agreement, or Customer Guidelines that help clients understand your level of security, the length of time you maintain backups, on-site and off-site, for their convenience.

This endears you to the client—making it much more difficult for a competitor to get their foot in the door. Declaring your business standards up front helps build confidence and loyalty in your organization, something that is ultimately more important to long-term clients, which are the clients you are most interested in doing business with.

> "The best way to keep client files safe is to backup. I'm a backup fanatic. Have firewalls, virus checkers, spam checkers. Save files to hard drive, backup to other computer's hard drive, and to CD or flash drive. Then the CDs and Flash are stored in the safe."
>
> Kathy Mandy, Select Word Services

Keeping client files safe also requires you to make sure that no one has the ability to access a client's files on your hard drive(s). Make certain you have up-to-date virus protections, firewalls, spam controls, spyware and adware detection, and removal software in place to further protect your clients and their files. Make certain they know and understand why you do so, and why you encourage them to protect themselves from these dangerous computer security issues that could damage their hardware and software.

Online storage options are also a great way to maintain all of your software, files and documents in a secure area that is easily accessible in case of an emergency...remember, your hard drive can crash, too! Communicating these tools to your clients helps them feel confident that they have chosen the right person to handle their tasks. They can rest assured that you can always access their files, when needed, while keeping them safe from damage and loss.

Your job is not only that of a service provider, but as a knowledgeable business partner who has your client's best interests in mind at all times. You will find surrounding yourself with like-minded business professionals is the best way to continually communicate your ethical business practices. These will be the people you'll use as references to potential clients, vendors and peers. If you have built solid relationships with ethical businesses, you're sure to be chosen over competitors who have not.

> "I backup my files daily to an external hard drive and I also burn CD's at the end of each month and keep these in a safe."
>
> Linda Siniscal, Third Hand Secretarial Service™

Maintaining Confidentiality

You might think that we've already covered most of the confidentiality issue, but there's still one more area of confidentiality that's an important part of your business ethics practices...the confidentiality not only of files, but of ideas.

If you don't have something in your contracts or agreements that includes proprietary information and ideas, consider addressing them. Although you should probably consider maintaining your work product ownership until the client has paid for the work product you developed, clients still need to know that you would not consider using any work product they paid for in order to benefit another client.

Maintaining the confidentiality of a client's work product, plagiarism, and intellectual property is probably the hardest type of ethical practice to address—and for many to understand. This makes it one of the most important areas to clearly define.

Running and operating a business is really difficult and requires lots of time and effort...time and effort for which we are not directly compensated. Clearly defining your standards as it relates to these areas will tie up your business ethics package in a way that communicates that you have achieved the highest level of ethical standards known to the business community.

Let's say that you create a marketing piece for a client in Albuquerque, and another client in Boston asks for the same type of marketing piece. They represent and sell to different industries, what possible harm could it be to use the same verbiage and layout for this second client, and either save yourself some time, allowing you to make a little more money, or charge the second client much less money for having produced the same result?

The answer is two-fold. First of all, it's not fair to the first client to have paid for the creation of a piece that client two will benefit from. It would also be unfair to the second client for you to charge them for time you didn't actually use to create their marketing piece, or leave them with the impression that you can create such a top-quality piece for such a minimal price. The next time you're asked to create a similar piece, the client will think that you padded your bill...why would this second, similar piece take so much more time to create? No matter how you spin it, there is no right way to do something so wrong and unfair.

Take your time in developing and implementing an ethical plan that covers all aspects of your practice and continue to develop the plan as your business evolves. Take some time to read more specifics on business ethics plans and guidelines in order to create a comprehensive program that will take your business to the next level, and help you throughout your business career. Developing good ethics takes lots of practice, and must be continually discussed and considered to keep in tune to the ethical demands that a business continually faces. Make sure you have clients, associates and peers in place to turn to when an ethical decision needs to be made.

Try using these three standard questions to help you make the best decision for your situation.

1. Is it legal? Not just by civil laws, but by business standards and company policy.
2. Is it fair to everyone? Does it give a distinct advantage to one party over the other?
3. How will I feel about the decision if I had to relay it to the world? How would I feel about myself, and the effect on the other party?

It's also significantly important to bounce your options off someone else who you feel can understand and whose opinion and ethics you can trust. Make sure that you aren't considering your emotional stake in the situation, this is not personal—it's business. Removing your emotions from the situation is important in the decision-making process. You may need to "sleep on it" and postpone making a decision until you've gained some distance and can give the solution enough thought and consideration.

Don't be afraid to ask a client to let you consider your options and get back to them. If they don't respect your desire to make an informed decision, they're probably not your equal in ethical standards. This could help you ultimately make the decision that works best for all...even if that decision means that you let them walk away without paying you for the work you already completed.

If a client is found to have unethical standards, you should not imagine that they would use good ethics in communicating the situation to others. It's a much smaller price to pay, not being paid for your work, than it would be to sever the relationship and part friends. The damage to your reputation, whether it's true, or not, is not something you should be willing to accept. Always take the high road, even when it might financially hurt to do so. It is much more likely that your business will outlast someone who doesn't subscribe to same level of ethical business practices you employ.

The Executive Summary

Developing and maintaining good ethics is one part of the equation; the other is communicating them to your client. You can do this in contracts and your company literature. Your clients are counting on you to be their partner and equal; so don't let them down.

Some business situations will test your ethics. Sometimes the right decision takes some thought. Ask yourself the three questions outlined in this chapter to help you make the right decision. Being an ethical virtual assistant will keep your practice thriving for the years to come (and you'll sleep better too!).

Chapter Links and Resources

Ethics Organizations & Resources	http://www.ivaa.org/
	www.business-ethics.org
	www.web-miner.com/busethics.htm
	www.ibe.org
	www.societyforbusinessethics.org
	www.crmlearning.com/ethics/
	www.media-partners.com
	www.character-ethics.org/?trackcode=bizcom
	www.ethicsweb.ca/resources/business/
	www.pdcnet.org/
	http://e-businessethics.com/
Online File	www.godaddy.com

Storage Options

www.streamload.com

www.freewebspace.net

www.all-the-free-space.com

www.filesanywhere.com

www.shadowstorage.com

www.box.net

www.mozy.com

www.carbonite.com

Chapter Nine

Growing Your Business

Once you've been in business for a little while and your practice is "full," you may decide you want to take your business to the next level. But, to grow, you will need to make some changes.

For some VAs, growth will mean going deeper into their specialization. For others it means adding staff and taking on more work. In this chapter, you'll learn how you can grow your business and take your professional career to the next step.

Adding Staff

You can't clone yourself. In order to take on more work, you will need to add more personnel to your team. While you can add substantially to your bottom line by doing this, you may also find yourself with more headaches. Not everyone is cut out for managing other people, but the VAs who don't mind it find the effort worth it.

Perhaps you started your practice as a generalist and have now evolved into a specialist. You may have "old" clients that want services you no longer wish to provide Using subcontractors or employees could offer you the option of continuing to maintain your "old" clients' business, and profits, while allowing you to focus on your specialization.

What if the response from your marketing efforts attracts clients looking for services you don't provide? Subcontractors and/or employees could be the answer to satisfying client needs, and adding a new cost center to your business tool belt.

What about a well-established client who is in need of services you've never provided, but they look to you for guidance in finding someone with the skills needed to complete the project? Although you could refer them to someone in your network, many times clients trust in your experience and understanding of their needs and prefer that you handle the project supervision and include the costs on your invoice. Subcontractors or employees would offer you the option to meet the client's demands, and make a profit in the process.

In some cases, you may prefer to create a referral network of talented VAs who can handle client projects that don't meet your business criteria, where the VA receiving the referral pays you a percentage of the total client invoices for a specific period of time, or they pay you a specific referral fee for each client you provide them.

For many VAs, managing their business, handling sales, and training and supervising subs or employees allows for the best growth and profit level for their growing practice.

Deciding between subcontractors and regular employees depends largely on your work volume, your needs and the level of risk you are comfortable with. No matter which you choose, adding additional help can provide for the long-term growth and success of your practice.

How to Effectively Work With Subcontractors

Subcontractors refer to temporary, independent workers who you would hire to help you with a project on a temporary basis. Much like you are to your clients, subcontractors are NOT your employees.

When working with, or as, a subcontractor, you need to take some additional points under consideration. If you are providing work to a sub-contractor, you still need to make a profit. You are the one that still has to check the work of the subcontractor, take the exposure for invoicing the client and receiving payment, and continue your marketing efforts for your practice, which brought in this overflow business in the first place. If you're looking for subcontractor work, remember that you may need to consider accepting less than your full hourly rate. Keep in mind that the VA is providing you with work you would not normally have access to; they are guaranteeing you get paid and it's their reputation on the line.

> "I don't want the responsibility of keeping an employee busy, trained, etc. When I'm too busy (or not available due to vacation or other commitments), I would much rather refer overflow work to an associate, and receive a 10% referral fee from them."
>
> Marsha Wagner, CastleVisions

Many subcontractors take offense at VAs who suggest they consider a discounted rate to do their subcontracting projects. Think of it as if you were working in the corporate world. If you were being paid $10.00 per hour to type their client's letters, if that client was only charged $10.00 per hour, how could they afford to pay your employment taxes and benefits; or pay for equipment, supplies, and utilities? It's really much the same when considering subcontractor projects. The VA who has secured the project must make some sort of profit, or they could not afford to outsource the project. If this still doesn't seem like a good option for you, look for VAs who might offer their overflow business in a referral model where you would pay a percentage, or a set fee, for accepting the client referral.

Qualify Your Subs

When considering subs, make sure you have a solid interview and/or testing program in place to make sure that the sub shares the level of expertise needed, and that they agree with your business practices and ethics. This will go far in helping you to build a long-lasting relationship that will be a win-win for both of you. Create and implement a Subcontractor Agreement that outlines your relationship and gives the subcontractor a clear picture of your confidentiality policy, payment terms, non-compete considerations, and whether or not they should have direct contact with your client. This is extremely important in finding and keeping talented subs. If you anticipate using subs on a regular basis, you may want to give them a small "test project" to see if they are able to meet your deadline and quality requirements BEFORE you give them a big, important client project.

When communicating projects to subcontractors, be as detailed as possible so that you're sure the project will be completed to the client's standards. Don't assume that they'll know that this client prefers their documents be typed in Arial 12-point with 1-inch margins all around, if it's not something you've discussed. Set reasonable deadlines that allow you extra time to proof the project before submitting it to your client. Good subcontractors many times can help you meet a client's quick turnaround time, but if ALL of your projects have short deadlines, it will be very difficult to keep good, talented subcontractors on your team.

One important key in working with subcontractors is your ability to pay for their services within an agreed upon time frame—whether or not the client has yet paid, or ever pays for the completed project. This is extremely important in dealing fairly with subcontractors and creating a situation that encourages subs

> *"Working with subs is great as long as they are a clone of yourself: honesty, integrity, same values, understand they are representing you, etc. Having subs or employees is not for everyone so pursue cautiously and educate yourself."*
> Sue Kramer,
> Peace of Mind Virtual Assistance

to keep deadlines and give your overflow work the priority it needs. Make sure that you're in a position to cover payment even under the most severe of situations, when a client fails to make good on payments. As a subcontractor, make sure that you treat the VA providing the project work to you just as if they were any other client. If you desire to continue to build a relationship with them, and secure additional projects, they must feel as if you consider them as you would any other client, and not as fill-in work that you'll get to when you have time.

Working with subcontractors can be a great way to allow you to handle additional projects, or continue to market your business and network to effectively grow a profitable practice. Make sure subcontractors are the right fit for your practice, and they can help you build a stronger and more profitable business than you ever imagined.

Multi-VA Practice

As the industry has continued to evolve, a new business model has emerged. The Multi-VA practice is one that partners with other talented virtual assistants and includes them in the marketing of their business, on all levels.

Let's say you have built your practice and decided that you only want to take on a specific type of project. It's the type of work you love, but you have all sorts of business in other areas that still helps you stay profitable. Contracting with other virtual assistants to take over the other client business you've built is a great way to take your business to the next level.

In this business model, the team-member VA will most likely be in direct contact with your client, and the multi-VA practice owner usually manages the invoicing and payments from the client and to the sub-contractor, with a portion of the profits staying with the business owner to continue to maintain, grow, and market the business to keep workflow coming in to make it worthwhile for the team-member VA.

Many Multi-VA Practices use some sort of online project management platform to stay current with what projects are in the works and which projects are still to be completed. You may find that this type of business works best for someone who is better at the marketing and sales aspect of the VA practice, leaving the actual workload to the members of the multi-VA practice team.

This business model also allows you, as the owner, additional freedoms from the traditional time constraints of most businesses, and allows you to grow your business beyond the number of hours you could traditionally handle in a traditional VA practice, or even one that utilizes sub-contractors at some level.

Someone using sub-contractors who does not reveal their team members in some way, be it on your website, or in your marketing materials, would not fit the traditional aspects of a Multi-VA practice.

When You Need to Hire Others

Hiring employees, part time or full time, is an expensive and labor-intensive undertaking. As a VA, you have been educating clients about the costs involved in hiring staff, and the advantages working with an independent contractor, like a VA, might allow. The same holds true for VAs adding staff. You are paying much more than their hourly salary. Consult a CPA, or a payroll service to find out exactly what your exposure will be as it relates to taxes, insurance and benefits required by your particular state and/or city.

Employees will also require a computer, software, desk, supplies, and training. They'll need set hours, breaks, paid holidays, and all those things that you may recall from a previous corporate experience. Depending on the guidelines within your subdivision or municipality, you may not be allowed to employ someone to work in your home office, which means you will need to consider leasing or purchasing office space, thereby raising your overhead.

> *"I like having an employee who can handle a lot of the administrative things in the office and free my time for client work. It's also good to have someone to talk to and bounce ideas off of."*
>
> Barbie Dallmann,
> Happy Fingers Word Processing and Business Services

Make sure that you include all these expenses when updating your business plan to incorporate employees. All these costs must be taken into consideration when quoting project pricing to clients, or you won't be able to support your employee for long.

You must take steps to make certain that you have the right person for the job. This not only means having the interview and testing process setup to allow you to find the perfect employee, but also a complete and detailed job description that will assist candidates in understanding the skills you need to be the right fit for the position. Make certain that you ask for and contact their references. Taking extra care in finding the most skilled person will help minimize the time needed in training and implementing this new hire.

The ideal situation would be to utilize employees in your home-based operation before taking on the additional expense of renting space. This will help you understand what's involved in supporting a staff person and whether you really want to take your business in that direction. Assess your current workload and take the time to consider and outline inner-office projects for slow periods when client work may not keep your new employee busy. Unstructured downtime can deteriorate an employer – employee relationship very quickly and create a hostile working environment for everyone.

Hiring full-time or part-time staff is a huge undertaking and one that should not be taken lightly. Also remember that this employee will have both direct and indirect contact with your clients, so that person needs to produce great work and represent your company as another professional.

Other considerations to having your new hire function in your home-based environment are somewhat personal. Will you feel embarrassed if your home isn't straightened up, or clean? Do you trust leaving this person home-alone, so to speak, while you may be out on appointments, at networking events, or running errands? What happens if you're not feeling well and want to take a sick day? What happens when you go on vacation for an extended period of time? Is the office closed? Do you expect the staffer to work from their home during these times? Imagine how this might work for you in a real life setting before you make the decision to consider this as your best option for hiring additional support for your growing business.

"I've worked with employees and now subcontractors since the inception of my business. It has allowed me to handle a large variety and volume of work that a solo-practitioner would not be able nor have the experience in handling. Our flexibility has allowed me to network and approach businesses with high volume requirements because I knew we could handle the workload and meet deadlines."

Sharon Williams,
The 24-Hour Secretary

Once you've found the right fit, take time to properly train your employee. Your new employee comes to you with a clean slate. Even though it may just be the two of you, unless you've taken the time to do so prior to hiring an employee, use them to help you create an Employee Manual to include everything employee related, such as work hours, holidays, pay schedule, review process, as well as a complete outline of your business model and ethics. An Employee Manual will go a long way in keeping this employee and any future employees on task, and provide them with an understanding of how you work and how they fit into the growth of your business.

When You Need to Move Out of Your Home Office

Although there are a few things, such as hiring employees, which may necessitate a move to leased space, moving from your home office will most likely be a personal preference.

You may find that working at home didn't provide you with the advantages you had hoped, and having leased space gives you the structure you need to move your business forward. Maybe you've developed your local clientele to a point that dropping off and picking up projects is an important element in your business process. This may lend itself more readily to an outside office for security and/or keeping your office hours manageable.

Perhaps you thought your "dream" business model was to stay at home with your children, only to find that you were unable to stay focused on either task; your business or your family. Handling client projects, managing childcare, getting children and family members to understand and adhere to personal/business schedule, or finding quality time to spend with your family are all issues that might be served better by having an outside office. Outside space considerations force you to get specific with the needs of your business and family, while allowing you to maintain a professional level of service for your clientele, and children or spouses may be able to discern what is your "work" and "home" time.

Need outside space, but don't feel your business income will allow it? Talk to local businesses, perhaps even your clients, and consider bartering your services in exchange for the use of some of their office space, or discuss renting a portion of their office. This will minimize your costs and exposure to the added terms a lease could bring to you.

Growing your business through the use of employees, subcontractors, a Multi-VA practice, or leased space can allow you to quickly propel your business to the next level, or create a situation that could just as quickly cripple your business and cause profits to take a nose-dive. Before taking any of these important steps in the future of your practice, make sure it will be a solid fit for your business style and specialization. Seek advice from qualified business, legal, and accounting professionals to make sure the time is right and you implement the right venue for your business success. Don't forget to use your peers and mentors to assist you in these endeavors. They are sure to give you a different perspective and help you decide on the necessary steps to make the right choice for the well-being of your practice.

Growth Doesn't Always Involve Volume

While the above ideas all show you how to grow your business by way of taking on additional projects, clients, and subcontractors or staff, business "growth" can be measured in other ways.

Go Deeper into a Niche

Perhaps you've decided that the type of work you were doing isn't satisfying you anymore, you want to work solely for clients in a specific industry, or just work on one type of skill (i.e. association management, website design, writing services, etc.)

Remember, just because you have had a client for a while, doesn't mean you have to keep that person forever. If the work you're doing for that client no longer fits your preferences, it's okay to let that client go to focus on others, which will give you more satisfaction. If at all possible, the best scenario would be to offer that client alternative suggestions for someone else to handle their business. Refer them to a specific peer, or website such as IVAA.org, where they can research your replacement. Never burn a bridge; you never know who that client could potentially refer you to who might fit into your new specialty.

Growth, in this sense, is about personal satisfaction and getting more joy out of what you do. Plus, when you become more specialized, either vertically (within an industry), or horizontally (working for people in a specific job role), you no longer become a commodity and can demand higher rates. Considering this type of growth helps establish you as an 'expert' in your field. Prospects, clients and peers will see this as a positive move to providing top-notch support with a focused approach.

Become a Leader

If you're a "veteran" VA now (or when you become one), you can also take your career in a different direction—that of an "expert" VA. Maybe you'd like to become a public speaker, a media contact, or a VA coach or college instructor. This can be achieved by adding to your functionality within the business; a separate entity to create and manage while providing support to your current clientele through subs or staff; or by dissolving your VA practice in favor of focusing on this new business model. You can utilize many of the options provided earlier in this book to help you decide and structure this advanced VA option.

This option may also involve another company name, website, marketing materials, business plan, etc., before you take on this option, make sure you have taken the time to plan and detail all the checks and balances that this may create for your current VA practice, as well as, this new business profile.

Teach Others How to Become Successful

Many colleges and junior colleges are beginning to offer virtual assistant tracts. If you like to teach, contact educational institutions in your area and explore teaching a class and sharing your knowledge with others.

As more and more people enter the VA field, some are looking for specialized coaching and instruction to make their business more successful and profitable—faster. As a coach, you could give them the inside track and instruction, based on your experience, to help them with their business.

One key to becoming an expert in your field is experience; not just as a VA, but one that has held a variety of industry-positions. Serving on the Board or a committee of a local or national VA organization can add legitimacy to your "expert" platform. Don't forget certifications, too.

Start small....get as much publicity as you can. Regularly write promotional articles and press releases to get more exposure. Offer to speak to associations or trade groups at their meetings about how they can benefit from VAs. You may end up speaking for "free" at first, but if you develop a valuable topic and refine your speaking skills, you should be able to move into paid gigs.

Some sites offer you a listing of your business designed for media people to contact an "expert" in your specific area. Included in your yearly subscription fee, some also offer free press release distribution. You'll be given some links at the end of the chapter.

The Executive Summary

Growing your business can take several different forms. Many VAs decide that adding employees or subcontractors allow them to take their business to the next level. However, it's not for everyone.

Others find that going deeper into their niche and referring out clients they aren't interested in keeping brings them higher billing rates and more job satisfaction.

Another avenue to take is becoming an educator. This can either take the form of an instructor at the college level, or a coach for new VAs. Sharing your experience and expertise with others can be very rewarding.

Finally, you can work at becoming an expert in your field. Would you like to be the one the media turns to when they want a quote? Would you like to speak in front of groups of people? These opportunities can be very exciting for the right VA and attainable with careful planning.

Change and growth is important to your business and keeps your life interesting. Whatever route you take, don't become stagnant. You are still in the early stage of an industry that will only get larger, more sophisticated, and respected with time. The sky is the limit and with the help and resources found in this book, we know, YOU CAN DO IT!

Chapter Links and Resources

Speaking Professionally

www.Toastmasters.com

www.nsaspeaker.org

www.speakersbureau.com

www.professionalspeakers.org

www.cityofexperts.com

www.conventionconnection.net

www.prospeakers.com

Epilogue – The Battle of Being a VA

Remote workers have long been a valuable resource to businesses of all sizes and shapes. Back in the early 80's, before the Internet existed, services ranging from basic administrative support to bookkeeping and consulting, were provided by people working from home. With the explosion of the Internet, the opportunity to complete tasks electronically cracked open the vault of 'virtual' workers.

The late 80's saw the inception of the Executive Suite, which allowed professional workers free office space in exchange for providing administrative support and telephone answering services to the tenants in an office complex.

By the early 90's, these pioneers were marketing themselves under the guise of Business Support Services providers, and while in most cases, their clients were within a 100-150 mile radius of their home or retail office space, the Internet opened them to a world they could never have imagined. There were no barriers to the potential client base they could market their services to, and by the mid-to-late '90's someone coined the term, "Virtual Assistant" as a catch-all for this style of remote support services provider.

Some VAs who entered this industry during the late 90's have always believed that the Business Support Services providers who only serviced local clients, or who used methods other than the Internet (electronically), should not look to promote themselves as a Virtual Assistant.

We believe that anyone who provides services remotely to their clients—whether around the corner or around the globe—is a welcome addition to the VA community. We found very few VAs who were totally web-based, or whose client base was strictly provided outside their local venue.

Another argument in the VA community seems to stem from whether or not you should call yourself a 'consultant', a 'coach', or a 'specialist' in lieu of utilizing the term Virtual Assistant. We encourage you to be all of them. Virtual Assistants can be professional speakers, consultants, bookkeepers, admins, IT specialists, or website designers, providing a laundry list of products and services, but they can still be "Virtual."

To us, the term "Virtual" signifies that we serve clients outside the scope of our home-based or brick and mortar office space to a wide variety of industries and client types, as an independent contractor. Projects are provided to us through non-traditional means, whether electronically, by fax, diskette, CD, or snail-mail.

Perhaps re-establishing ourselves as providers of Virtual Assistance, rather than being a Virtual Assistant, will help to communicate a broader spectrum of what the VA has to offer. It's almost as if the term "administrative assistant" has a stigma attached to it of being a menial or less-than-professional occupation, as once happened with the now-seldom-used term 'secretary'.

Whichever side of the fence you find yourself on, know that there are no hard and fast rules to who should or who should not be considered a VA. The infancy of the industry may be what makes for such heated debates over something that seems a personal preference and not a topic for fisticuffs. There will always be debate, and always be those who are unwilling to consider a compromise.

As the industry continues to grow and become recognized, we believe that most everyone will be more open and willing to share the term Virtual Assistant. The key may be to continue to educate people globally on the benefits of being and using a VA to bring solidarity and support to this growing and evolving marketplace. As the industry becomes more recognized, it makes sense for you to tie your horse to the wagon of VA industry marketing, don't you think?

We encourage you to embrace the term VA and help educate others about the industry so that the next time you tell someone you're a VA, you will see the spark of recognition and knowledge that they know who and what you are. When we get the 'deer in the headlights' look; that should be a reminder that we need to educate on the advantages of working with a VA.

Happy Trails....

Epilogue

"Know why you are unique and know how to express that."
Michele Hanson-O'Reggio, A Virtual Pro

"Continually re-evaluate your business and personal life to make sure everything is the way you want it. If not, identify and make the changes you desire. Never lose confidence in yourself or your abilities. If you're having doubts, reach out to your peers for reassurance, advice and suggestions to keep going. Don't be afraid of failing or changing. Many are afraid of failing, the only failure is to stop trying, to give in, or to settle for less than you deserve."
Janice Wlodarski, Professional Publishing Services

"Do what you love and the money will follow. If there are aspects of your job that you really hate, then find a way to do something else. Negative feelings burn up your energy, they drag you down, and keep you from realizing your full potential."
Barbie Dallmann, Happy Fingers Word Processing and Business Services

"I believe the biggest keys to success in any entrepreneurial venture are enthusiasm, believing in yourself and your service and lots of hard work. We can all provide the services in which we specialize – entrepreneurship is really so much more than that."
Sandy Giusti, Consider it Done Virtual Assistant Services

"Find ways to build trust in relationships with other VAs and businesspeople. Trust is key, sometimes even more important than skill."
Judy Vorfeld, Office Support Services

"Don't give up. It took four years for my business to reach the point where I felt comfortable leaving my full-time job. It was a scary time, but I knew if I offered the best services that I can to my clients, my business would succeed. You also must keep in constant communication with your clients and ask for feedback. Taking feedback is sometimes not an easy thing to do, but it is the only way you can grow as an individual. Networking is my last piece of advice. There are many worthwhile local and national organizations to join and network, network, network. Also, become involved, attend meetings, volunteer for committees – it can only help you in the long run."
Linda Siniscal, Third Hand Secretarial Service™

"FAITH, IMAGE, NETWORK, BELIEVE & STRETCH! Remember, this is your company and you can grow it to your wildest dreams or restrict it with fear and a negative attitude. The only one who can stop you is you. Surround yourself ONLY with those who are where you want to be. Leaders are those who keep trying and develop a little thicker skin over time. Owning a business is not easy or everyone would do it."
Sue Kramer, Peace of Mind Virtual Assistance

"Understand that building a business is a journey. It won't happen overnight, but it will happen...if you're very proficient at what you do and if you're willing to hang in there through the rough start-up period. Be sure that you're creating a career that is satisfying for you, professionally, emotionally and financially. Pay yourself a regular salary and make sure you're providing for your retirement. If you can't afford to do that, you may need to take a hard look at your rate structure. Remember – it's okay to make money!"

Heather Lee, design/type

"Always make sure to scrutinize your skill set before accepting a new project. If it's not something you're great at, refer it to someone else. Don't be money hungry and take jobs just because you need the $. Make sure the project and the client appeals to you on some level or it will soon feel like drudgery."

Katie Baird, Loose Ends

"Be professional. Know that to make money, you have to spend money. Being the lowest priced provider puts you out of business in a snap. Don't be afraid to ask prospects lots of questions, and don't be afraid to set parameters around your business. Remember, it's your business, not your client's business. If they tell you how to work, how to set prices, how to do the job, how many hours to work, etc., you might as well get a job with benefits."

Kathy Mandy, Select Word Services

"Enjoy what you do and who you work with. One of the best parts of working for yourself is that 'you' get to decide how far you will go, and what sort of business you will shape!"

Vicki L. Duncan, Duncan Business Services, Inc.

Survey Results

As a part of our research for this book, we contacted more than 75 established Virtual Assistants in different areas of the world, in different specialties, as well as generalists, who were at different stages of their entrepreneurial career, and asked them if they'd be willing to participate in our adventure by answering a survey about their businesses and the virtual assistance industry.

Of the more than 75 contacted, 23 replied and agreed to participate. You have already seen some of the wisdom and insights they have provided, throughout the book, and you will find their bios and contact information later in this section.

Below is an outline of some of the general information that was compiled as a result of our questions:

I. Years in Business?

Average of all 23-participants	8.96 years
Least time in business	1-year
Most time in business	25-years

Years in Business	Number of Participants	Years in Business	Number of Participants
1	2	13	1
2	2	14	0
3	1	15	2
4	2	16	0
5	2	17	1
6	3	18,19,20	0
7, or 8	0	21	1
9	1	22,23	0
10	0	24	2
11	1	25	1
12	1		

II. **Generalist or Specialist?**
   Generalists   13
   Specialists   10

III. **Started Full or Part-Time?**
   Full-time   13
   Part-time   10

IV. **How long Part-time before going full-time?**
   6 months   1
   1 year   3
   1-5 years   1
   2 years   1
   3 years   1
   4 years   1
   5 years   1

   Still maintain part-time practice   0
   Considering choosing part-time   1

V. **Do they have a Business Plan?**
   Yes   12
   No   11

VI. **How business organized**
   Sole Proprietorship   17
   Limited Liability Company   1
   C-Corporation   2
   S-Corporation   3

VII. **Do they have a website?**
   Yes   19
   No   4

VIII. **How do they track personal time & appointments?**
   PDA   2
   Outlook   2
   No response   2

IX. **How do they track client time?**
Manually   10
Trax Time or Time Stamp   7

X.   **Best most effective form of marketing?**
Word of mouth   14
Networking   5
Website   3
Yellow Pages   1

XI. **Do they serve local clients?**
Yes   22
No   1

XII. **Do they hold Certifications?**
Yes   12
No   11

XIII. **Are they Home Based?**
Yes   19
No   4

IXX. **Have they ever had employees?**
Yes   4
No   19

XX. **Have they ever worked with sub-contractors?**
Yes   18
No   5

Based on this sampling of VAs, we find:
- The Virtual Assistance Industry is growing rapidly and although the Internet has accounted for much of this explosion, the industry has been around for some time (25 years or more) under the guise of Business Support Services;

- There are slightly more generalists than specialists (57%-43%);
- There are slightly more full-time than part-time VAs (57%-43%);
- Of the 43% of VAs who start out part-time, all eventually go full-time, 90% of which are full-time within the first 2-years;
- Almost half have a business plan; and half do not;
- 74% are organized as Sole Proprietors;
- 83% have a website;
- 17% of the respondents responded to how they track personal time and 50% of them use a PDA, 50% use Outlook;
- 74% of the respondents responded to how they track client time and 59% track it manually, while 41% utilize time-tracking software;
- The best form of Marketing is Word of Mouth (61%);
- 96% of respondents have local clients;
- 52% hold industry Certifications while 48% do not;
- 83% are home-based;
- 83% have never had employees; and
- 78% have worked with sub-contractors.

In our opinion, this data helps solidify certain facts. Virtual Assistance is a viable, profitable, home-based business option, most of which are organized as a Sole Proprietorship. Having and developing a website, and developing opportunities for word-of-mouth marketing are vital to your success. More VAs are starting their practices full-time, while most that start part-time are able to transition to a full-time business within the first two years. If we are to say that having a business plan is important to your business, we have a long way to go in communicating and educating VAs on the importance and advantages of having one. Industry Certifications do hold some importance in growing a practice (52% of respondents hold certification designations), and most VAs choose a sub-contractor relationship over hiring employees.

Survey Participants Bios

Katie Baird
Loose Ends – www.LooseEnds.net
ktcosmose@LooseEnds.net
928-445-4724

Katie has operated Loose Ends, which provides executive and personal assistance services, since 1997. Her clientele includes businesses, schools, nonprofit agencies and individuals. Her specialties are web development, desktop publishing/layout, and project management. She enjoys the challenge of pulling together all the components of a complex project, hence the name of her company. As part of the exciting new field of Virtual Assistance, she serves a number of her clients from afar, without ever having met face-to-face.

Barbie Dallmann
Happy Fingers Word Processing & Business Services –
www.HappyFingers.com
Barbie@happyfingers.com
304-345-4495

Lori Davis
Davis Virtual Assistants – www.davisva.com
lori@davisva.com
917-319-8224

Lori Davis is the Director of the Future at Davis Virtual Assistants, a New York-based Virtual Assistance firm. DavisVA provides a wide array of administrative, technical and creative solutions to a broad spectrum of business owners, doing so with the highest level of customer care and the most competitive rates in the VA industry. To learn more about Lori and Davis Virtual Assistants, please visit their website outlined above, or
http://loridavis.typepad.com/davisva.

Vicki L. Duncan
Duncan Business Services, Inc. – www.dbsicolorado.com
vduncan@dbsicolorado.com
970-622-8018

Duncan Business Services, Inc. provides a broad range of business and marketing support services to help its clients with special projects, overflow and outsourcing needs. DBSI is owned and operated by Vicki L. Duncan and is located in Loveland, Colorado. Vicki has more than 30 years of experience in business administration, and holds a bachelor's degree in Speech Communication from the University of Northern Colorado, as well as associates degrees in Business Education and Legal Secretarial Services.

Jackie Eastwick
Allison Lane Business Solutions – www.allisonlane.com
Jackie@allisonlane.com
856-228-7430

Nina Feldman
Nina Feldman Connections – www.ninafeldman.com
Nina@ninafeldman.com
510-655-4296

Owner since 1981 of Nina Feldman Connections, a business-support/referral service based in Oakland, California, Nina frequently coaches VAs on startup and pricing. She is committed to helping VAs value their services and get paid what they're worth.

Sandy Giusti
Consider It Done Virtual Assistant Services – www.consideritdonebest.com
sandy@consideritdonebest.com
781-365-1072

Sandy became a Virtual Assistant after 15 years in the broadcast radio business. She held administrative positions throughout her radio career, ending with Executive Assistant to the CFO, and prior to being laid off in 2000.

Michele Hanson-O'Reggio
AVirtual Pro - www.AVirtualpro.com
Michele@avirtualpro.com
866-851-8225

Michele O'Reggio is an IVAA Certified Virtual Assistant (CVA) providing administrative and online marketing services to coaches, consultants and solo entrepreneurs.

Lisa Hoffman
Premier Administrative Services – www.premieradminservices.com
lisa@premieradminservices.com
847-265-5363

Over 20 years of progressive, dynamic and hands-on business achievements, ranging from small businesses to Fortune 500 Corporations. Successful positions include Executive Assistant, Office Manager, Inside & Outside Sales, Marketing & Sales Coordinator and Customer Service Specialist. With Premier Administrative Services, there are no worries associated with interviewing, overhead or commitment!

Survey Participants Bios

Heather Jacobson
Valley Virtual Assistants – www.valleyva.net
Heather@valleyva.net
540-904-2505

Heather Jacobson of Valley Virtual Assistants has over 12 years experience in the administrative field, specializing in marketing, sales, and new business development. She strives to cater to small businesses, allowing her skills to shine in her practice. During Heather's corporate life, she held various positions, including executive assistant, marketing research specialist, research director, and director of sales promotions research, at various television stations across the country. Heather's skills are not limited to the aforementioned, as she also excels in Internet research, website design, copy writing, editing and proofreading, and is extremely proficient in numerous software and hardware applications.

Sue Kramer
Peace of Mind Virtual Assistance – www.vapeaceofmind.com
Solutions@vapeaceofmind.com
630-323-3886

Sue Kramer is president and founder of Peace of Mind Virtual Assistance, a company she started in 2003 in Clarendon Hills, IL. Peace of Mind Virtual Assistance provides virtual office assistance to professionals in the Chicago area. She has more than 20 years of experience in administrative support, purchasing, and project coordination.

Heather Lee
Design/type
disgntype@aol.com
651-407-2618

Heather Lee is the principal of design/type, a business support services firm established in 1988. The company specializes in desktop publishing, presentation design, research, writing and editorial services, and transcription. An active member of industry associations, Heather is the founder and past-president of the Minnesota Association of Business Support Services. She has authored articles on a variety of industry-related topics and has been a featured speaker at numerous national and regional conferences, seminars and workshops.

JudyAnn Lorenz
Bar JD Communications
absolutewest@yahoo.com
417-543-4447

Kathy Mandy
Select Word Services
swskm@aol.com
952-470-0465

Select Word Services began in November 1981 and offered general secretarial services. Over time, and due to health reasons, the business has evolved to providing transcription services to researchers, writers, editors, and media producers. Kathy Mandy grew the business by building long-term relationships with her clients, which has led to a loyal customer and referral base. Though technology has changed over the last 25 years, Kathy's focus has remained on customer services.

Marlene McCall
Creative Office Services – www.officeservices911.com
marlene@officeservices911.com
510-649-1295

Faye Partridge
Partridge Typing & Print, Ltd.
Fayep@xtra.co.nz
++64-3-578-4777

Faye commenced business in 1982, when the second of her three sons was three months old, in response to a new businessperson (an accountant), who was moving to the district and needed someone to provide typing services. Faye originally ran the business from home and now operates from a commercial location in town. She has expanded the range of services, in response to demand and to stay abreast of the market; however, the main core of the business is still word processing. She never set out to be in 'business', when simply answering the call to help; however, things evolved, and she is still there, keeping her business small enough to maintain hands-on services and the 'personal touch'.

Linda Siniscal
Third Hand Secretarial Service™ - www.yourextrahand.com
Linda@yourextrahand.com
732-899-0810

Linda Siniscal, owner of Third Hand Secretarial Service™, has been offering bookkeeping services, as well as administrative support, to her client base, since 1994. Her clients include coaches, speakers, non-profits and other small business owners, many of whom have been clients since she launched her business. Linda provides a variety of administrative tasks, which are tailored to her client's needs. A member of IVAA since its inception, she is certified by the State of New Jersey as an SBE and WBE company. Linda is currently serving on the Board of Directors for IVAA (2005-2008) and is also a member of NAWBO, Association of Professional Bookkeepers, and the Delaware Valley Virtual Assistants Association. Prior to starting her business, Linda was an executive assistant to the Treasurer of an international steel company and office manager/bookkeeper for a heavy highway construction company.

Kimberley Thomas-Catanzaro
Bookkeeping & Secretarial Services www.on-linesecretary.com
kthomas@on-linesecretary.com
561-741-2139

Bookkeeping and Secretarial Services is located in Jupiter, Florida. Kim's experience includes over 15 years of office and bookkeeping experience. She has worked in various capacities. She offers experience in the fields of individual and small business bookkeeping, office management, secretarial skills, telecommunication skills, executive assistance, credit and collections services, temporary assistance and virtual assistance.

Judy Vorfeld
Office Support Services – www.ossweb.com
Judyvorfeld@ossweb.com
623-876-8168

Judy has been in office support services since 1992 and moved into Web development in 1998. Judy offers Web development, webmastering, consulting, editing, writing, and photography: mostly (but not exclusively) for the small business community.

Marsha Wagner
CastleVisions – www.castlevisions.com
Marsha@castlevisions.com
612-338-2122

Marsha Wagner created CastleVisions in 1993, with the stated mission of encouraging and empowering people to make choices and changes that lead to greater joy – making their dreams come true. She does this by helping them build solid foundations upon which to grow. Over the years, service areas have evolved to include, but are not in any way limited to, the following areas: desktop publishing and design; basic and enhanced word processing; spreadsheet design and data entry; business consulting; and event and conference planning. In keeping with the CastleVisions concept, Marsha decides which projects to accept on a case-by-case basis. If it sounds fun, she'll try it; if it's not, she won't do it again!

Sharon Williams
The 24 Hour Secretary – www.the24hoursecretary.com
Sharon@the24hoursecretary.com
410-521-7001

Sharon is a full-time, practicing Virtual Assistant, who opened her business in November 1990. She has a B.A. in Business Administration and Labor Relations, Master Virtual Assistant (MVA) and Professional Real Estate Virtual Assistant (PREVA) designations, and serves as Chairperson of the Alliance for Virtual Business (A4VB). Her business passion is public relations and marketing, and, in this capacity, she has appeared on international, national, and local network TV, radio and Internet shows, as well as in the print media. She has published three books, two on Marketing Your VA Practice and one on Small Business Marketing, and a booklet each on Branding, Effective Press Releases and Pitch Letters that Get Results. She enjoys networking, reading, writing, playing card games and walking with her Black Labrador, Domino. Her personal passion is her granddaughter, Brittany, who is an aspiring runway model. She travels with her on modeling jobs, takes her to classes, and, overall, just enjoys her time with her. Brittany keeps her young!

Janice Wlodarski
Progressive Publishing Services – www.propubservices.com
ppservices@tampabay.rr.com
813-719-9181

Janice Wlodarski opened her VA business in 1999. She has a BA in Business Administration and has more than 20 years experience in the corporate environment. Ms. Wlodarski's areas of expertise include desktop publishing and graphic design, and electronic document preparation and management. Her clients include entrepreneurs, non-profit organizations, coaches and multi-national companies. She is a certified Master Virtual Assistant (MVA) and a member of the American Business Women's Association (ABWA).

Caroline Wright
The Wright Solution
CLW@wrightsolution.com
609-564-0449

The Wright Solution specializes in marketing, transaction and listing management, and business building for real estate agents.

BASIC WORK FOR HIRE AGREEMENT:

WORK FOR HIRE AGREEMENT

This Work for Hire Agreement ("Agreement") is made this _____ day of March, _____, between **Your VA Practice**, and **Proposed Client, Inc.** having its principal place of business at **123 MAIN STREET, ANYWHERE, FL 35344**. In this Agreement, the party who is contracting to receive the services shall be referred to as the "Client" and the party who will be providing the services shall be referred to as Your VA Practice.

1. **DESCRIPTION OF SERVICES.** Beginning on **Today's date**, **Your VA Practice** will provide consulting and project services, as designated by the Client. Because of the "virtual" nature of our relationship, some services may be provided by phone and/or e-mail. The Client understands that they will be invoiced for the time utilized by phone, e-mail, or in person, when client projects are discussed, or consultation is provided.

2. **PAYMENT FOR SERVICES.** The Client will pay compensation to **Your VA Practice** for these services, based on the hourly rates, as agreed upon. This compensation shall be payable upon receipt of invoice. Any invoice disputes/discrepancies must be addressed within 10 days of the original invoice date.

3. **TERM/TERMINATION.** This Agreement may be terminated by either party upon written notice to the other party, within five days of signing of the Agreement.

4. **RELATIONSHIP OF PARTIES.** It is understood by the parties that **Your VA Practice** is an independent contractor with respect to the Client and not an employee of the Client. The Client will not provide fringe benefits, including health insurance benefits, paid vacation, or any other employee benefit, for the benefit of **Your VA Practice**.

5. **WORK PRODUCT OWNERSHIP.** Any copyrighted works, ideas, discoveries, inventions, patents, products, or other information (collectively, the "Work Product") developed in whole, or in part, by **Your VA Practice**, in connection with the Services, shall be the exclusive property of the Client, once payment for the Work Product has been made. Upon request, **Your VA Practice** shall sign all documents necessary to confirm or perfect the exclusive ownership of Client to the Work Product.

Page One of Two.

6. **PROOFREADING & REVISIONS.** Prices include light proofreading by **Your VA Practice**, including checking for errors in grammar, punctuation, and spelling. A draft of Client's documents shall be furnished to Client for proofreading, and the final copy printed only after the Client approves the draft. Typographical errors shall be corrected at no additional charge; however, revisions made by the Client shall be billed at regular hourly rates.

   Final responsibility for proofreading and approving the final draft lies with the Client. **Your VA Practice** *cannot be held liable for typographical omissions, content, etc., after final approval by Client.*

7. **CONFIDENTIALITY/TRADE SECRETS. Your VA Practice** will not at any time or in any manner, either directly or indirectly, use for the personal benefit of **Your VA Practice**, or divulge, disclose, or communicate in any manner, any information that is proprietary to the Client. **Your VA Practice** will protect such information and treat it as strictly confidential. This provision shall continue to be effective after the termination of this Agreement.

8. **AGREEMENT MODIFICATION:** No modification, termination or attempted waiver of this Agreement, or any term thereof, shall be valid, unless it is in writing and signed by the party against whom the same is sought to be enforced.

9. **ENTIRE AGREEMENT.** This Agreement contains the entire agreement of the parties, and there are no other promises or conditions in any other agreement whether oral or written.

10. **SEVERABILITY**. If any provision of this Agreement shall be held to be invalid or unenforceable for any reason, the remaining provisions shall continue to be valid and enforceable. If a court finds that any provision of this Agreement is invalid or unenforceable, but that by limiting such provision, it would become valid and enforceable, then such provision shall be deemed to be written, construed, and enforced as so limited.

Party contracting services:

By: _____

Service Provider:

By: _____
    Jane Doe, President
    Your VA Practice

RETAINER AGREEMENT:

CLIENT RETAINER AGREEMENT

This agreement ("Agreement") is made and entered into by and between
Company Name: _____, referred to as
"The Company"
Company Address: _____
_____
_____

AND

Contractor Name:_____, referred to as
"the Contractor"
Contractor Address: _____
_____
_____

All parties agree as follows:

1. **The Services.** The Contractor shall provide:
   - *List services here*

2. **Compensation and Payment.** The Company shall compensate the Contractor for the Services in the amount of $_____. Payments to the Contractor shall be made on a bi-monthly basis and will be due on the first and fifteenth of each month. Each payment will be in the amount of $_____. Accordingly, the Contractor is not required to submit time records to the Company. The Contractor will, however, be reimbursed for any long-distance phone charges directly related to services provided to The Company.

3. **Benefits.** The Contractor shall not participate in any benefit plan or program of the Company, including, but not limited to, health insurance, life insurance, disability insurance, pension or profit sharing, workers' compensation, paid vacation or sick pay.

4. **Service Location.** The Service to be provided by the Contractor under this Agreement shall be performed at the Contractor's place of business. (provide address)

5. **Schedule and Days Off.** The Contractor has agreed to be available to provide services during normal business hours. Monday – Friday 8am – 5pm EST, excluding national holidays, for the duration of one year from this date: _____ . The following are additional days in which the Contractor will not be available to offer services:
   - *List any regular holidays or vacations here*

6. **Licenses.** The Contractor shall, at his or her sole cost and expense, secure and maintain in effect continuously throughout the term hereof, any licenses necessary concerning the performance by the Contractor of the Services.

7. **Compliance with Laws.** The Contractor shall provide the Services in accordance with all applicable laws, ordinances, and contracts.

8. **No Violation.** The Contractor represents, warrants and agrees that the performance of the Services will not violate any contractual rights, trade secrets or other rights of any third party.

9. **Term and Termination.** Either party may terminate this Agreement, without cause, upon thirty (30) days prior written notice to the other party. Provided, however, that each party may terminate the Agreement immediately without prior notification in the event of a breach of this Agreement by the other party. In the event of termination or expiration, the Contractor shall be paid Contractor's usual compensation, up to the effective date of termination.

10. **Nondisclosure and Nonsolicitation.** The Contractor shall not directly, or indirectly, disclose to any person, other than a representative of the Company, at any time either during the term of this Agreement or following the termination or expiration thereof, any confidential or proprietary information pertaining to the Company, including but not limited to, customer lists, contacts, financial data, sales data, supply sources, business opportunities for new or developing business, plans and models, or trade secrets. Furthermore, the Contractor agrees that during the term of this Agreement, and for a period of one year following the termination or expiration of this Agreement, the Contractor shall not directly or indirectly solicit or attempt to solicit any customers or suppliers of the Company, other than on behalf of Company.

    11. **Independent Contractor Status.** The Contractor and the Company agree that the Contractor shall, at all times, be an independent contractor, and that no relationship of employer and employee, partners or other relationship is created, or intended to be created, by this Agreement for any purposes, including without limitation for federal and state tax and other state and federal purposes. The Contractor assumes full responsibility for payment of all federal, state and local taxes imposed or required under unemployment insurance, self-employment, social security and income tax laws, upon compensation paid to the Contractor. The Contractor shall not hold himself or herself as an employee, partner or agent of the Company. The Contractor acknowledges that he or she has duly signed and returned to the Company Form W-9, and all compensation paid to the Contractor under this Agreement will be reported annually to the Internal Revenue Service on Form 1099, of which the Contractor shall receive a copy.

12. **Indemnification of Company.** The Contractor shall indemnify the Company against all liability, loss or damages, including consequential and incidental damages, and against all claims or actions based on or arising out of damage or injury (including death) caused by or sustained in connection with the performance by the Contractor of the Service, or based on any violation of any statute, ordinance, regulation or contract, and the defense of any such claims or actions, including attorneys' fees. The Contractor shall also indemnify the Company against all liability and loss in connection with, and shall assume full responsibility for, payment of all federal, state and local taxes or contributions imposed or required under unemployment insurance, social security and income tax laws, with respect to the Contractor's performance of this Agreement.

13. **Miscellaneous.** This Agreement contains the entire understanding of the parties with respect to all matters referred to herein, and may not be changed, amended, modified or waived orally, but only by a written agreement signed by the party against whom enforcement of any waiver, change, modification, or amendment is sought. This Agreement shall be construed under the laws of the State of (Your State) and (Your County), (Your State). If any provision in this Agreement is held by a court of competent jurisdiction to be invalid, void, or unenforceable, the remaining provisions shall, nevertheless, continue in full force and effect. The headings to the sections of this Agreement are for reference only and shall not affect its construction or interpretation.

14. **Notices.** Any notice, request, demand, consent, waiver or other communication, which either party may wish to serve, or may be required to serve, on either party, shall be in writing and shall be served by personal delivery, by facsimile, by prepaid recognized overnight air express delivery, by pre-paid certified mail, return receipt requested, or by pre-paid telegram addressed to such party at the address set forth at the beginning of this Agreement.

IN WITNESS WHEREOF, the parties have executed this Agreement on this ____ day of _____, _____ and will continue in effect until it's expiration one year from this date on the ____ day of _____, _____.

COMPANY: (Sign)_____ (Print) _____
Address: _____ Apt # _____
City: _____ State: _____ ZIP: _____
Home Phone: (___) _____ Fax Phone: (___) _____
Social Security Number (or FIN): _____ - _____ - _____

CONTRACTOR: (Sign)_____
(Print)_____ (Title)_____
Address: _____ Apt # _____
City: _____ State: _____ ZIP: _____
Office Phone: (___) _____ Fax Phone: (___) _____

EDITORIAL RETAINER AGREEMENT:

YOUR VA PRACTICE
EDITORIAL RETAINER AGREEMENT

This Work-for-Hire retainer agreement is dated _____, and made between **ABC Company, of 123 Main Street, Anytown, USA** and **Your VA Practice**, whose address is **345 Main Street, Anytown, USA**, and concerns ongoing editorial support services for ABC Company.

1. **SERVICES INCLUDED:** Client agrees that Your VA Practice will perform editorial assistant services and other related services, as agreed upon by both parties.

2. **FEES:** The fee for the included services in Section 1 is $x per month, which includes up to 40 hours of monthly services. Phone consultations are part of the monthly time allotment. Client will be invoiced on the 15th of the month for services to be provided the following month. Payment can be made via check, money order or Paypal, and must be paid on or before the first of the month for that month's services.

3. **SERVICES NOT INCLUDED:** The client's hourly rate includes general overhead expenses. Any client-specific expenses will be billed to the client. These may include: postage, online subscriptions or services, professional printing fees, resource books or subscriptions, etc.

4. **TERMS OF CONTRACT:** This contract will continue until such time as either party gives a minimum of 30-days written notice of termination.

5. **CONFIDENTIALITY:** Your VA Practice agrees not to convey confidential information to any outside parties.

6. **COLLECTIONS:** If payment is not received before the first day of the month Your VA Practice is scheduled to provide service, Your VA Practice's services will be suspended until account is brought current with no adjustment to the client's monthly retainer fee. Any attorney fees, court costs, or other costs incurred in collection of delinquent accounts shall be paid by Client.

7. **ERRORS AND OMISSIONS:** Client bears responsibility for final proofreading and final approvals, prior to the completion of all projects. Your VA Practice will not be held liable for errors and omissions overlooked by the client in the final approval draft.

Page One of Two.

IN WITNESS WHEREOF, the parties have signed this agreement on the date first appearing.

Signature_____ Print Name_____ Date_____

Title_____ Telephone_____ Email_____

Signature_____ Print Name_____ Date_____

Title_____ Telephone_____ Email_____

CONFIDENTIALITY AGREEMENT:

CONFIDENTIALITY AGREEMENT

This Confidentiality Agreement (this "Agreement") is made effective as of today's date, between **Your VA Practice**, of **456 Main Street, Anytown USA** and **Ms. Potential Client** of **Potential Client Company, 345 Main Street, Anytown, USA**.

In this Agreement, the party who owns the Confidential Information will be referred to as "**Your VA Practice**," and the party to whom the Confidential Information will be disclosed will be referred to as "**Jane Doe**."

Your VA Practice is engaged in editing, ghostwriting, and editorial assistance services for non-fiction authors and entrepreneurs. **Jane Doe** is engaged in freelance editing, ghostwriting, and other marketing communications tasks. Information will be disclosed to **Jane Doe** so she can assist **Your VA Practice** with editing, ghostwriting, research, and transcription **Your VA Practice** has requested that **Jane Doe** will protect the confidential material and information which may be disclosed between **Your VA Practice** and **Jane Doe**. Therefore, the parties agree as follows:

   I. **CONFIDENTIAL INFORMATION.** The term "Confidential Information" means any information or material, which is proprietary to **Your VA Practice**, whether or not owned or developed by **Your VA Practice**, which is not generally known other than by **Your VA Practice**, and which **Jane Doe** may obtain through any direct or indirect contact with **Your VA Practice**.

      A. Confidential Information includes, without limitation:
- business records and plans
- customer lists and records
- trade secrets
- products
- inventions
- product design information
- pricing structure
- computer programs and listings
- copyrights and other intellectual property and other proprietary information.

   II. **PROTECTION OF CONFIDENTIAL INFORMATION.** **Jane Doe** understands and acknowledges that the Confidential Information has been developed or obtained by **Your VA Practice** by the investment of significant time, effort and expense, and that the Confidential

Information is a valuable, special and unique asset of **Your VA Practice**, which provides **Your VA Practice** with a significant competitive advantage, and needs to be protected from improper disclosure. In consideration for the disclosure of the Confidential Information, **Jane Doe** agrees to hold in confidence and to not disclose the Confidential Information to any person or entity for a period of ten years after the effective date of this Agreement, without the prior written consent of **Your VA Practice**. In addition, **Jane Doe** agrees that:

i. *No Copying/Modifying.* **Jane Doe** will not copy or modify any Confidential Information, without the prior written consent of **Your VA Practice**.

ii. *Application to Employees.* Further, **Jane Doe** shall not disclose any Confidential Information to any employees of **Jane Doe**, except those employees who are required to have the Confidential Information in order to perform their job duties in connection with the limited purposes of this Agreement. Each permitted employee to whom Confidential Information is disclosed shall sign a non-disclosure agreement, substantially the same as this Agreement, at the request of **Your VA Practice**.

iii. *Unauthorized Disclosure of Information.* If it appears that Jane Doe has disclosed (or has threatened to disclose) Confidential Information in violation of this Agreement, **Your VA Practice** shall be entitled to an injunction to restrain **Jane Doe** from disclosing, in whole or in part, the Confidential Information. **Your VA Practice** shall not be prohibited by this provision from pursuing other remedies, including a claim for losses and damages.

III. **RETURN OF CONFIDENTIAL INFORMATION.** Upon the written request of **Your VA Practice**, **Jane Doe** shall return to **Your VA Practice** all written materials containing the Confidential Information. **Jane Doe** shall also deliver to **Your VA Practice** written statements signed by **Jane Doe** certifying that all materials have been returned within five (5) business days of receipt of the request.

IV. **RELATIONSHIP OF PARTIES.** Neither party has an obligation under this Agreement to purchase any service or item from the other party, or commercially offer any products using or incorporating the Confidential Information. This Agreement does not create any agency, partnership, or joint venture.

V. **NO WARRANTY**. **Jane Doe** acknowledges and agrees that the Confidential Information is provided on an AS IS basis. **Your VA**

Practice MAKES NO WARRANTIES, EXPRESS OR IMPLIED, WITH RESPECT TO THE CONFIDENTIAL INFORMATION AND HEREBY EXPRESSLY DISCLAIMS ANY AND ALL IMPLIED WARRANTIES OF MERCHANTABILITY AND FITNESS FOR A PARTICULAR PURPOSE. IN NO EVENT SHALL **Your VA Practice** BE LIABLE FOR ANY DIRECT, INDIRECT, SPECIAL, OR CONSEQUENTIAL DAMAGES IN CONNECTION WITH, OR ARISING OUT OF, THE PERFORMANCE OR USE OF ANY PORTION OF THE CONFIDENTIAL INFORMATION. **Your VA Practice** does not represent or warrant that any product or business plans disclosed to **Jane Doe** will be marketed or carried out as disclosed, or at all. Any actions taken by **Jane Doe** in response to the disclosure of the Confidential Information shall be solely at the risk of **Jane Doe**.

VI. **LIMITED LICENSE TO USE. Jane Doe** shall not acquire any intellectual property rights under this Agreement, except the limited right to use set out above. **Jane Doe** acknowledges that, as between **Your VA Practice** and **Jane Doe**, the Confidential Information, and all related copyrights and other intellectual property rights, are (and at all times will be) the property of **Your VA Practice**, even if suggestions, comments, and/or ideas made by **Jane Doe** are incorporated into the Confidential Information or related materials during the period of this Agreement.

VII. **GENERAL PROVISIONS.** This Agreement sets forth the entire understanding of the parties regarding confidentiality. Any amendments must be in writing and signed by both parties. This Agreement shall be construed under the laws of the State of (**Your State**). This Agreement shall not be assignable by either party, and neither party may delegate its duties under this Agreement, without the prior written consent of the other party. The confidentiality provisions of this Agreement shall remain in full force and effect after the effective date of this Agreement.

Information Owner:
Your VA Practice

By: _____
Mary Smith, Proprietor

Recipient:
Jane Doe

By: _____
Jane Doe, Proprietor

TWO SUBCONTRACTOR AGREEMENT:

SUBCONTRACTOR AGREEMENT

This Subcontractor Agreement (the "Agreement") is made this ___ day of _____, 200_ (the "Effective Date"), by and between **Your VA Practice**, and **Jane Doe, Sub's VA Practice** (the "Subcontractor") with its principal place of business at: **123 Main Street, Anytown, USA**.

1. **General Purpose**: **Your VA Practice** provides services and has contracted with a third party to perform various other services, as needed. **Your VA Practice** desires to retain Subcontractor, and Subcontractor accepts retainment by **Your VA Practice** as an independent contractor upon the terms and conditions of this Agreement.

2. **Relationship of Parties:** Subcontractor is an independent contractor, and neither Subcontractor nor their employees are, or shall be, deemed as **Your VA Practice**'s employees. This Agreement does not create any agency or partnership relationship. In its capacity as an independent contractor, Subcontractor agrees and represents **Your VA Practice** as follows: Subcontractor has the right to perform services for others during the term of this Agreement, subject to non-competition provisions set out in this Agreement. Subcontractor has the sole right to control and direct the means, manner and method by which the services required by this Agreement will be performed; Subcontractor will furnish all equipment and materials used to provide the services required by this Agreement, except to the extent that Subcontractor's work must be performed on or with the Client's computer or existing software; Subcontractor is responsible for paying all ordinary and necessary expenses of its employees; **Your VA Practice** shall not provide any insurance coverage or any kind for Subcontractor or its employees; and **Your VA Practice** shall not withhold from Subcontractor's compensation any amount that would normally be withheld from any employee's pay.

3. **Nature of Work:** Subcontractor will perform consulting and project services for **Your VA Practice**'s clients. The details of such services will be set forth in an initial consultation with an outline of the project, which will detail the estimated time necessary to complete the project and the compensation to be paid to the Subcontractor for such services. When necessary, Subcontractor will accept work direction from Client-supervisory personnel.

4. **Payment:** Your VA Practice will pay Subcontractor at the rate specified in the initial consultation and project outline. Subcontractor will submit an appropriate invoice to cover the approved hours/costs of the project. Subcontractor will receive payment within fourteen (14) days of receipt of invoice and completion of project to **Your VA Practice**'s satisfaction.

5. **Duration:** This Agreement commences on the date outlined above and will remain in effect indefinitely. This Agreement may be terminated by either party upon fourteen (14) days written notice to the other party.

6. **Assignment:** Acknowledging that the services to be performed under this Agreement are unique and personal, Subcontractor may not assign any of his/her rights or delegate any of his/her duties or obligations of **Your VA Practice** under this Agreement. The rights and obligations of **Your VA Practice** under this Agreement shall ensure to the benefit of, and shall be binding upon the successors of, **Your VA Practice**.

7. **Taxes:** Subcontractor will be solely responsible for applicable taxes, withholding, insurance and other payments due as a result of performing services herein. Should Subcontractor require a yearly 1099, they must provide Your VA Practice with a completed W-9 for reporting to the Internal Revenue Service.

8. **Materials:** Subcontractor shall furnish, at Subcontractor's own expense, all labor, materials, equipment and other items necessary to carry out the terms of this Agreement, subject to facilities and equipment furnished to Subcontractor (i.e. Client provides necessary hardware, software and other materials as needed).

9. **Confidentiality/Trade Secrets:** In connection with Subcontractor's work with **Your VA Practice**'s Clients, it may be necessary for Subcontractor to have access to information which is confidential or proprietary to **Your VA Practice**, its Clients or its prospective Clients. Subcontractor understands and agrees that all such information provided by **Your VA Practice** or the Client is confidential and proprietary and will be held by the Subcontractor in strict confidence. Subcontractor agrees not to directly contact the Client for any reason, unless by permission of **Your VA Practice**. Subcontractor will not provide, disclose or make available any such confidential or proprietary information to any third party, except as necessary to perform its duties hereunder, and Subcontractor shall be responsible for the actions of its employees, consultants and contractors relating to the confidential information. All information concerning the

existence of this Agreement and the existence of any business relationship between Subcontractor, **Your VA Practice** and the Client shall be kept in complete confidence. Subcontractor will not disclose to **Your VA Practice** information or material that is a trade secret of any third party. The provisions of this Section 9 shall survive any termination of this Agreement.

10. **Ownership:** Subcontractor hereby assigns to **Your VA Practice** and Client its entire right, title and interest in the Work Product including all patents, copyrights, trade secrets, trademarks and all other proprietary rights in, or based on, the Work Product (for purposes of this Agreement "Work Product" means all graphics, drawings, video, materials, animation, audio works, software program systems, data and materials, in whatever form, first produced by or for Subcontractor as a result of, or related to, performance of work or services under this Agreement and each work project). Subcontractor shall execute and aid in the preparation of any papers that **Your VA Practice** may consider necessary or helpful to obtain or maintain any patents, copyrights, trademarks or other proprietary rights, at no charge to **Your VA Practice**, but at **Your VA Practice**'s expense. **Your VA Practice** shall reimburse Subcontractor for all reasonable out-of-pocket expenses so incurred.

11. **Covenant Not to Compete:** Subcontractor agrees that during the term of this Agreement, and for a period of twenty-four (24) months after termination of this Agreement, Subcontractor will not directly or indirectly, whether as an employee, independent contractor or subcontractor, provide any data processing, consulting or placement services to the individual Clients or departments for which Subcontractor has performed services through **Your VA Practice**.

12. **Agreement Modification:** No modification, termination or attempted waiver of this Agreement, or any term thereof, shall be valid, unless it is in writing and signed by the party against whom the same is sought to be enforced.

13. **Entire Agreement:** This Agreement contains the entire agreement of the parties, and there are no other promises or conditions in any other agreement, whether oral or written.

14. **Severability:** Whenever possible, each provision of this Agreement will be interpreted in such manner as to be effective and valid under applicable law. If any provision of this Agreement is held to be invalid, illegal or unenforceable under applicable law, such provision will be ineffective only to the extent of such invalidity, illegality, or unenforceability, without invalidating the remainder of this Agreement.

Page Three of Four.

Your VA Practice

By: _____
Mary Brown, Owner

Subcontractor:

By signing this document, I acknowledge my authority to do so on behalf of the organization I represent.

By: _____
Signature

_____   _____
Print name   Position with Organization

SUBCONTRACT AGREEMENT:

SUBCONTRACT AGREEMENT

This subcontract Agreement is entered into this day of **TODAY'S DATE** in the **City of Anytown, State of Anystate**.

Subcontractor, **Jane Doe**, hereinafter called "Subcontractor," agrees to provide the following:
Up to 5 hours per week of administrative assistance for an anonymous client. Duties include email screening, database management and mailings with the preferred style and other preferences previously provided to **Jane Doe** by **Mary Brown**.

Owner(s) Name: **Mary Brown**, d/b/a **Your VA Practice**

Owner(s) Address: **456 Central Ave, Anytown, USA**

Prime Contractor, **Mary Brown**, hereinafter called the "Contractor," agrees to pay to the Subcontractor for the satisfactory performance of the Subcontractor's work the sum of (**x**)/hr in accordance with the following terms and conditions:

DESCRIPTION OF WORK (describe labor, materials and equipment to be furnished):
Email screening, database management and mailings on a weekly basis (5 hours per week). The subcontractor will be paid (**x**)/hour for satisfactory completion of the work.

SCOPE OF WORK: All work necessary or incidental to complete work for the project, in strict accordance with this subcontract and all terms and conditions hereof.

OTHER SPECIAL PROVISIONS: Under no circumstances may the Subcontractor release the name of this anonymous client to any outside parties, or contract will be immediately terminated.

LENGTH OF CONTRACT: This contract is effective from today's date until a minimum of two weeks notice is given by either party.

SCHEDULE OF PAYMENT(S): Billing is to be sent to **Your VA Practice** on a biweekly basis and payment will be made by contractor within 15 days of receiving the subcontractor's invoice.

This schedule of payment(s) is strictly construed and is not conditional upon Contractor(s) first being paid by client.

Page One of Two.

Any amounts that are not paid by the contractor, when due, shall bear interest at a rate of 1 1/2% per month until paid, or the maximum rate permitted by law, whichever is higher.

TIME AND SCHEDULING WORK: Subcontractor is responsible for completing the 5 hours of work by noon Eastern, on Fridays. The necessary files may be sent to contractor as they are completed.

SOLE AGREEMENT: This Agreement, including all terms and conditions hereof, is expressly agreed to and constitutes the entire Agreement as of this date. No other Agreement or understandings, verbal or written, expressed or implied, are a part of this Agreement unless specified herein:
  Confidentiality Agreement
  Non-Compete Agreement

IN WITNESS HEREOF, the parties have accepted this Agreement the day and year first above written.

Subcontractor Name: **Jane Doe**   EIN number: **12-1112343**

Subcontractor Address: **123 Main Street, Anytown, USA 12333**

_____

Subcontractor Signature

Contractor Name: **Mary Brown, Your VA Practice**

Contractor Address: **456 Central Ave, Anytown, USA**

_____   _____

Contractor Signature   Title

NON-SOLICIATION AGREEMENT FOR SUB-CONTRACTORS:

NON-SOLICITATION AGREEMENT

This Non-Solicitation Agreement (this "Agreement") is made effective as of **Month, Day, __06,** by and between **Your VA Practice, LLC of 456 Main Street, Anytown, USA 12345,** and **Jane Doe** of **Jane Doe LLC, 123 Main Street, Anytown, USA, 12345.**

In this Agreement, the party who is requesting the non-solicitation from the other party shall be referred to as "**Your VA Practice LLC**," and the party who is agreeing not to solicit shall be referred to as "**Jane Doe**."

Jane Doe is a virtual assistance practice who will be providing subcontracting services for **Your VA Practice, LLC**.

1. **NON-SOLICITATION COVENANT**. For a period of three years after the effective date of this Agreement, **Jane Doe** will not directly or indirectly solicit business from, or attempt to sell, license, or provide the same or similar products or services, as are now provided, to any customer or client of **Your VA Practice LLC**.

2. **ENTIRE AGREEMENT.** This Agreement contains the entire agreement of the parties regarding the subject matter of this Agreement, and there are no other promises or conditions in any other agreement, whether oral or written.

3. **SEVERABILITY**. The parties have attempted to limit the non-solicitation provision so that it applies only to the extent necessary to protect legitimate business and property interests. If any provision of this Agreement shall be held to be invalid or unenforceable for any reason, the remaining provisions shall continue to be valid and enforceable. If a court finds that any provision of this Agreement is invalid or unenforceable, but that by limiting such provision it would become valid and enforceable, then such provision shall be deemed to be written, construed, and enforced as so limited.

4. **INJUNCTION.** It is agreed that if **Jane Doe** violates the terms of this Agreement, irreparable harm will occur. Therefore, **Your VA Practice LLC** will be entitled to seek injunctive relief (i.e., a court order that requires **Jane Doe** to comply with this Agreement) to enforce the terms of this Agreement.

5. **APPLICABLE LAW**. This Agreement shall be governed by the laws of the State of **Your State.**

Page One of Two.

PROTECTED PARTY:
Your VA Practice LLC

By: _____
   Mary Brown

NON-COMPETING PARTY:
Jane Doe

By: _____
   Jane Doe

SAMPLE BUSINESS PLAN:

EXECUTIVE SUMMARY

I. Mission

The Mission of ABC Company is to provide top quality and timely website development and support services to businesses of all kinds requiring such services on an 'as needed' basis.

II. The Company

ABC Company was founded in 2000 and has provided website development and support to clients, as well as, continually educating ABC's staff on the latest developments and technologies, as it relates to website development. It is a Sole Proprietorship and offices are located in Anytown, TX.

III. Business

ABC Company provides professional services to support clients in need of a new website, or who might need to update or maintain their current site.

We are in the start-up phase of our business, having just set up our office and developed a marketing plan. We expect to achieve $2,000 per month in sales and pretax profits in 2000, and achieve $35,000 in sales and pretax profits by 2001.

IV. Service

ABC Company will provide the following services:
- Website consultation
- Website development from start to finish or as required
- Assistance in domain registration
- Website Hosting
- Search Engine Optimization (SEO)
- Upload to the World Wide Web
- Maintenance and periodic updates, as needed

V. The Market

Our business has endless potential. Through carefully placed advertisements online and in magazines and periodicals targeting specific market segments, such as small businesses, home-based businesses, sole proprietorships, and even local Chambers and civic groups, we can build a prosperous business.

Although we have many competitors, our research indicates that not many website designers can offer the full package of services, and/or be willing to offer individual services that will be key to building a client base.

Through strategic Internet and local networking, speaking, referrals and article submission discussing the industry and website advantages, we feel we will be able to place ourselves as the 'experts' in our field.

VI. Competition

Local direct competition is not as widespread as our web-based competition, but we will be using our diverse knowledge and strengths to increase the probabilities of securing a larger market share of available business. Further research and networking will provide additional focus on our competitive edge.

VII. Risk/Opportunity

The greatest risk we have in our business today would be a pricing risk. We feel we can overcome this risk through communication, knowledge, training, and creative samples that will allow us to be a major force in providing top-notch services to a huge market potential. We believe there is plenty of business out there, and with our high quality and level of service, we will attain a large market share.

VIII. Goals

Staffing – to be achieved by January 2001

As the business grows, we will continue to interview and train additional support staff to be able to groom them to handle our incoming clients. We anticipate utilizing independent contractors (at least two) in the first year, with a reassessment of needs by the end of 2002.

Equipment
- Server
- Two-desktop PC's; two-desktop MAC's; two laptop computers
- Software – Dreamweaver and Front Page
- Business Software – QuickBooks; MSOffice 2003 Professional
- Toll-free phone line; dedicated phone line; DSL connection

Continuing Education
- Web design courses twice per year
- Graphic design courses twice per year

Training
- Establish program materials for training staff
- Establish program materials for online training programs

Page Two of Three.

Organizations
- National Website Designers Association
- Local and National Chamber of Commerce
- IT Professionals Association of America

NOTE: The above sample is what could be used for any virtual service business. Your business plan should always be a work in progress. Update it at least annually as your business continues to evolve. If you're considering financing you will also need to include capital requirements (how much funding you'll need); financial plan (where you are financially today); a current sales summary; and a balance sheet summary.

TRACKING CLIENT PROJECT TIME:

Client Weekly Time Record For Week Ending: __ __/__ __/__ __

Client: _____

Date	Time In	Time Out	Time In	Time Out	Total	Project

DAILY TIME RECORD

Date: __ __/__ __/__ __

Project	Qty. Done	Time Start	Time Stop	Billable Time	Type of Work

SAMPLE DOCUMENTS

DAILY TIME & EXPENSE RECORD

Date: __ __/__ __/__ __

Hour		Client	Description of Service	Rate/Hour	Postage, materials, other expenses	Total Time
	:10					
	:20					
	:30					
	:40					
	:50					
	:10					
	:20					
	:30					
	:40					
	:50					
	:10					
	:20					
	:30					
	:40					
	:50					
	:10					
	:20					
	:30					
	:40					
	:50					
	:10					
	:20					
	:30					
	:40					
	:50					
	:10					
	:20					
	:30					
	:40					
	:50					
	:10					
	:20					
	:30					
	:40					
	:50					
	:10					
	:20					
	:30					
	:40					
	:50					
	:10					
	:20					
	:30					
	:40					
	:50					

About the Authors

Jeannine Clontz
Accurate Business Services

Jeannine Clontz owner of Accurate Business Services specializes in marketing and social media support, training and consultation to busy entrepreneurs. Jeannine finds Realtor and Speaker/Coach/Consultant support to be an important niche in her practice, although she provides support to clients in all industries. Jeannine's passion and research in the area of business ethics has led to a speaking and writing career on the subject. She has written and published articles on business ethics for the IVAA Cast in 2003/2004, and speaks on business ethics nationwide.

Her company Accurate Business Services was established in August of 1998. Not long after starting her business, Jeannine joined IVAA (International Virtual Assistant Association, one of the organization's first 30 members.

Jeannine is a writer, author and speaker on many business topics, including ethics, and recently started a Virtual Assistance Coaching program (http://www.VABizCoach.com). This book received rave reviews and is being utilized by several community colleges nationwide as a part of their business curriculum. Jeannine also teaches the course at several St. Louis area community colleges and a non-profit organization, Connections to Success which helps and supports disadvantaged women and men looking to re-enter the workforce.

She is an IVAA CVA (Certified Virtual Assistant), EthicsChecked™, CRESS (Certified Real Estate Support Specialist), PREVA (Professional Real Estate VA), CRVA (Certified Realtor.com VA), and MVA (Master VA).

She is the winner of the 2001 Bill Williams' Business Person of the Year Award; 2002 Arnold Kiwanis Distinguished Service Award; 2003 Don Earl Citizen of the Year Award; 2007 Kirkwood Des Peres Area Chamber of Commerce Volunteer of the Year; the 2005 and 2007, Metro St. Louis WCR (Women's Council of REALTORS) Affiliate of the Year; the 2009 Small Business Administration (SBA.gov) Home-Based Business Champion for the St. Louis District; 2009 NAWBO (National Association of Women Business Owners) St. Louis Chapter's Member of the Year; and the 2009 Thomas Leonard International Virtual Assistant of Distinction.

Jeannine is a very committed volunteer and supports community activities which include:

- Arnold Chamber of Commerce (3-years on the Board, Vice-President 2001, and President 2002);
- Arnold Kiwanis (Past President; club newsletter 2-years);
- A.N.E.W. (A Network for Empowering Women – Treasurer 2-years, chair all committees);
- Mentor-Workforce Preparation @ Jefferson Community College (5 years);
- Jefferson College Curriculum Advisory Council 2004 through 2010
- Arnold Optimist Club (Charter Secretary);
- IVAA (International Virtual Assistants Assn.) member 7-years, served on the committee to upgrade the CVA (Certified Virtual Assistant) exam, Bylaws committee 2001 & 2003, and Bylaws Committee Chair 2004, VP, 2004-2005, and served as Board President 2005-2006, and 2010-2011;
- JOIN-N (Jefferson County Online Information Network) Past Outreach Committee Member;
- Fox Warrior Stadium Club (Past Secretary/Treasurer 3-yrs.);
- OSN (Office Support Network – Past President 2-yrs.);
- Fox and Windsor Elementary Schools Guest Reader Program;
- ESPW (Encouraging, Supporting, Promoting Women)volunteer, VP/President-elect St. Louis Chapter (2005), and President 2006
- NAWBO (National Association of Women Business Owners) Board member (5-years), Chairperson PR Committee; Co-Chair Communications (2-years); Treasurer (1-year); and President 2011-2012;
- eWomenNetwork PR Chair (3-years); and
- Women's Council of Realtors (WCR) – Board member & Newsletter Chair 2005 & 2006; Secretary 2007-2008.

Her client base includes small to medium sized businesses, entrepreneurs, real estate professionals, authors, professional speakers, coaches, consultants and home-based business owners.

She believes in continuing her education and regularly attends local and online classes to sharpen her skills, keep up-to-date on current technologies, and increase her knowledge of the specific software needs of her clients.

Her vast background in customer service, administrative support, sales and purchasing provides a unique skill-set to offer mentorship, guidance, and VA support to clients, associates and peers.

For more information, visit Accurate Business Services on the web at: http://www.Accbizsvcs.com

email: Jeannine@Accbizsvcs.com

Phone: 636-282-9550 \ Fax: 636-282-9973

About the Authors

Lauren Hidden
Hidden Helper, LLC

Lauren Hidden, owner of The Hidden Helpers, is a professional writer, author, editor, writing coach and certified professional virtual author assistant. Working with professionals in a variety of industries, Lauren helps her clients get their messages across clearly, concisely, and persuasively.

Lauren has edited dozens of books, including memoirs, business books, and novels. While she enjoys all types of editing and proofreading, she's been told she has a special gift for content editing—ensuring the information is logical, flowing, and consistent.

Lauren has a Bachelor's Degree in Communications/Journalism from Shippensburg University. Before launching her own business, she worked in the public relations department of a Fortune 500 company and as a caseworker for the local agency on aging.

Lauren is a dedicated volunteer, recently serving as the Director of Research and Development and previously serving as the Marketing Director for the International Virtual Assistants Association (IVAA) and as the past Secretary for the Central Pennsylvania Association for Female Executives. She also occasionally guest teaches in local public secondary schools.

In addition to co-authoring *Entrepreneurial Freedom*, Lauren also co-authored *Write It Right: The Ground Rules for Self-Editing Like the Pros* with Dawn Josephson.

Lauren works with clients all over the U.S. and beyond, but calls the Harrisburg, PA area her home. When she's not working, she enjoys spending time with her husband and two sons, traveling, reading, and spending time with friends.

For more information, visit The Hidden Helpers on the web at: http://www.hiddenhelper.com

Email: Lauren@hiddenhelper.com

Phone: 866-669-0940

Index

Adding staff, 125
Advertising, 91
   Paid, 91
Agreement, 33
   Confidentiality, 156-158
   Non-solicitation, 165-166
   Retainer, 151-155
   Editorial, 138-139
   Sub-contractor, 159-164
   Work-for-hire, 149-150
Answering Machine, 27
Article writing, 44, 49, 67, 68, 87
Associations, 85-86
Author bios
   Jeannine Clontz, 175
   Lauren Hidden, 177
Bartering, 92, 131
Battle of being VA, 135
Blog(s), 48, 87, 92, 94, 97, 98, 99, 106
Bookkeeping Software, 30
   QuickBooks, 30, 32, 34
Books, 86
Brand(ing), 39
Brochures, 29, 36, 40, 50, 58
Budget, 27
   Website, 47
Business Cards, 56
   Name, 40
   Plan, 56, 57,58
Capabilities
   Representing, 118
Capital, 18, 19
Certifications, 84,
Challenges
   Balancing work and home, 109
   Boundaries, 109-110

   Isolation, 112-113
   Scheduling, 109-110
   Small children, 119-120
   Working from home, 109
Clients, 25, 26, 27, 32
   Communicating with, 71-72
   Criteria, 52, 53
   Difficult, 72
   Ethics, 74
   Finding, 63
   Firing, 76
   Keeping files safe, 119, 120
   Local vs. virtual, 73-74
   Networking, 63, 64, 65
   Overcoming objections, 68-69
   Saying 'no', 75
Collections, 77
Commercials
   30-second, 41-42
Communications, 29
Company Organization, 30
   Corporations (s-Corp, c-Corp), 31
   Limited Liability Company, 30
   Sole proprietor, 30
Computer, 28
Conferences, 83
Confidence, 21-22
Confidentiality, 120-121
Continuing Education, 22, 81-82
   Certifications, 84
Contracts, 33
   Confidentiality, 156-158
   Non-solicitation, 165-166
   Retainer, 151-153
   Editorial, 154-155
   Sub-contractor, 159-162, 163-164

Contracts (cont.)
   Work-for-hire, 149-150
Copier, 29, 36
Corporation, 31
Customer Service, 74
Difficult clients
   Handling, 72
Domain name, 46, 59
Economy
   Cutbacks, 17
   Downsized, 17
   Layoffs, 17
Elevator Speech, 41
E-mail
   Signature lines, 49-50
Epilogue, 135-136
Equipment
   All-in-one machines, 29
   Copier, 29
   Fax, 29
   Printers, 29
   Scanner, 29
Ethics
   Business, 117
   Confidentiality, 120
   Customer Service, 64
   Keeping files safe, 119
   Representing experience &
     capabilities, 118
Executive Summary, 167-169
Expenses, 18-19, 30, 34, 42, 50
Experience, 20
Fax, 29
   Online, 29
Fees
   Setting, 50-52
   Structure, 56

Financing, 18-19, 24
Forms, 33
   Tracking client time, 33, 37, 54-56
Full-time, 25-27
Funding, 20, 26, 27
Giveaways, 96-97
Growing your business, 125
   Adding staff, 125
   Become a leader, 132
   Develop a niche, 131-132
   Hiring employees, 129-130
   Office space, 130-131
   Teach others, 132-133
   Working with sub-contractors, 126
   Qualifying your sub, 127
Hardware, 28
Hiring staff/employees, 129-130
Home-based Considerations, 17
Hourly rate, 45, 46
Image
   Professional, 56-58
Income, 26, 27, 50
   Collections, 77-78
Infomercials
   30-second, 41
Inkjet printer, 29, 35
Internet
   Browsers, 48
   Presence, 42
Invoices, 30
Isolation, 112-113
Keeping client files safe, 119-120
Keywords, 47
Laserjet printer, 29, 35
Leads groups, 41, 64, 93
Letterhead, 36, 57
Limited Liability Company (LLC), 30

Logo, 39, 47, 49, 57
Marketing, 91
   Bartering, 92
   Brochures, 29
   Giveaways, 96-97
   Paid advertising, 91-92
   Sales, 95-96
   Social Media, 96
   Tracking, 92-93
   What works, 92
   Word-of-mouth, 93
Meta tags, 47
Multi-VA Practice, 128
Network, 21
Networking, 22, 35, 57
   How to, 63
   Leads groups, 64
   Online, 63
   Speaking, 63
   Writing articles, 67, 68
Niche, 131-132
Organizations
   IVAA, 33, 36, 37
Outgoing Personality, 22
Overcoming client objections, 68-69
Packages, 45
Part-time, 25-27
Payables
   Collections, 77-78
Peers, 21
Perseverance, 21
Planning, 25
Podcasts, 87
Pricing Structure, 44
   Industry Production Standards
     (ISP), 56

Printer, 29
   Color inkjet, 29, 35
   Laserjet Color, 29
Printing, 29, 58
Professional
   Associations, 85-86
   Certifications, 84-85
   Conferences, 83-84
   Development, 81
   Information on the Web, 87
   Podcasts, 87
   Programs, 81, 82
Promotional products, 93
Public Relations, 91
   Publicity, 94-95
Publicity
   Free, 94-95
Rates, 44-45, 50-51
   Industry Production Standards
     (ISP), 56
Record keeping, 34
Retail Space, 20
Retainer, 33
   Agreements, 151-155
Running a business, 23
Salary, 19
Sales, 95-96
Sample documents/contracts, 149-169
Scanner, 29
Search Engine Optimization (SEO), 98, 101, 105
Self-confidence, 22
Self-esteem, 23
Serving your clients, 25
Small Business Administration
   (SBA.gov), 33, 90

Social Media, 97
   Bookmarking, 97
   Facebook, 97, 98, 99, 104
   Groups, 100
   LinkedIn, 97, 98, 99, 100, 101, 102, 104
   Networks, 65-66
   MySpace, 97
   Plaxo, 98
   Twitter, 97, 98, 99, 100, 104
   Vimeo, 98
   YouTube, 98
Software, 28
   Bookkeeping, 30
      QuickBooks, 30, 32, 34
   Expenses, 30
   Fax, 29
   Time management, 34
   Transcription, digital 30
Sole Proprietorship, 30
Speaking, 63, 68
Start-up Costs, 27
Start-up options, 25-26
Sub-contractors
   Qualifying, 127
   Time management, 56
   Working effectively with, 126
Survey
   Participant bios, 143-148
   Results, 139-142
Tagline, 39, 41, 49, 56, 62
Telephone, 27

Time management, 54
   Client, 54
   Industry Production Standards (ISP), 56
   Software, 34
   Sub-contractors, 56
   To-do list 55
Transcription, 30
   Digital, 30
   Machines, 30
   Online systems, 30
Virtual Professional, 17
Voice Mail, 27, 28
Volunteering, 23
Website, 42-43
   Browsers, 48
   Creation, 42
   Domain name, 46
   Getting set up on the WWW, 46
   Hosting, 46
   Keywords, 47
   Meta tags, 47
   Pages, 43
   Rates, 44-46
   Signature lines, 49
Word-of-mouth
   Marketing, 93
Work at home
   Challenges, 109
   Isolation, 112-113
   Small children, 113-114

Made in the USA
Lexington, KY
14 March 2013